special education

NEXT STEP OF EDU.

Published by Dhayal Publication
Bairasar Rajgarh (Churu) Rajasthan

Book - Master Guide Special Education

Copyright © 2025 by Preetam Dhayal , Dhayal Publication

No part of this publication may be reproduced or distributed in any form or by any means, electronic, mechanical, photocopying, recording, or otherwise or stored in a database or retrieval system without the prior written permission of the publishers. The program listings   (if any) may be entered, stored and executed in a computer system, but they may not be reproduced for publications.

Author : Preetam Dhayal
Cover Design : Creative Designer

Contact us :
Whatsapp No. 9588082726
Mail : preetamdhayal@gmail.com

GRATITUDE

I am grateful to all the co-operation and encouragement I have received from my teacher, students, family members, staff, friends and library staff and others while writing this book. I have been able to accomplish this noble task especially because of the encouragement of my uncle Shri Rajendra Dhayal and the guidance of my father Shri Rajveer Singh Dhayal (Govt. Teacher).

PREETAM DHAYAL

1 Foundations of Special Education

- Concept, Meaning, and Scope of Special Education 🎓

- Historical Perspective of Special Education 🔘

- Difference between Special Education, Integrated Education & Inclusive Education 🏫

- Principles of Special Education 📖

- Role of Special Education in Mainstream Education 🔡

- **Responsibilities & Classroom Structure of Special Educator** 🧑‍🏫

2 Understanding Disabilities & Their Classification

- Definition & Classification of Disabilities (As per RPWD Act, 2016) 📜

- Sensory Disabilities: Visual, Hearing, Speech & Language Impairment 👀👂

- Physical & Locomotor Disabilities 🦽

- Intellectual & Developmental Disabilities (Intellectual Disability, Autism Spectrum Disorder, Learning Disabilities) 🧠

- Mental Illness & Psychosocial Disabilities 🤕

- Multiple Disabilities & their Educational Implications 🔄

- **Education of ADHD & Autistic Children** 🧠

- **Education of Mentally Retarded, Physically Handicapped & Hearing/Vision Impaired Children** 👶🧒

- **Education of Socially & Economically Disadvantaged Children** 🗄

---

3 Policies, Acts & Laws Related to Special Education

- Rights of Persons with Disabilities (RPWD) Act, 2016 📜

- National Education Policy (NEP) 2020 & Inclusive Education 📖

- The Rehabilitation Council of India (RCI) Act, 1992 🎓

- Sarva Shiksha Abhiyan (SSA) & Samagra Shiksha Abhiyan (SSA) 🏫

- Integrated Education for Disabled Children (IEDC) & Inclusive Education for Disabled at Secondary Stage (IEDSS) 🗄

- United Nations Convention on the Rights of Persons with Disabilities (UNCRPD) ⚪

- **All Acts, Organizations & Institutions Related to Special Education** 🏛

- **Schemes Related to Special Education (Central & State Govt.)** 🏢

---

4 Special Psychology & Psychological Support

- Meaning & Importance of Inclusive Education ⚪

- Barriers to Inclusion & Strategies to Overcome Them 🚧

https://www.specialeducationnotes.in

- Universal Design for Learning (UDL) & Its Implementation 🏫

- Role of Regular Teachers & Special Educators in Inclusion 👩‍🏫

- Individualized Education Program (IEP) & Its Components 📝

- Adaptations & Modifications in Curriculum & Teaching Methods 📖

- Multi-Sensory Teaching Approaches 👀👂

- **Types of Disorders: Developmental, Personality & Abnormal Psychology** 😷

- **Psychological Therapies: Cognitive Behavioral Therapy (CBT), Applied Behavior Analysis (ABA), Positive Behavior Support (PBS)** 💭

- **Occupational Psychology & Therapy** 🔄

---

5 Assessment & Evaluation in Special Education

- Types of Assessment: Formative, Summative, Diagnostic & Dynamic 📊

- Tools & Techniques Used in Special Education 🛠

- Standardized Vs Non-Standardized Assessments 📜

- Intelligence Tests: Wechsler Intelligence Scale for Children (WISC) 🧠

- Adaptive Behavior Scale: Vineland Adaptive Behavior Scale (VABS) 📊

- Functional Behavior Assessment (FBA) & Behavioral Interventions 😷

- **Assessment of Different Disabilities** 📋

---

6 Assistive Technology & Support Services

- Importance of Assistive Technology in Special Education 🤖
- Low-Tech, Mid-Tech & High-Tech Assistive Devices 📱
- Augmentative & Alternative Communication (AAC) Devices 🗣️
- Use of ICT in Special Education 💻
- Role of Resource Rooms & Special Schools 🏫
- Counseling Services & Family Support 🫂

7 Therapy, Treatment & Special Interventions

- **All Types of Therapy & Treatment for Special Needs** 🏥
- **Individualized Behavior Plan (IBP) & Behavioral Interventions** 🔄
- **Personalities in Special Education** 🧑 🏫

8 Role of a Special Educator

- **Identification & Early Intervention** 🧑‍🏫
- **Collaborating with Parents, Teachers & Therapists** 🫂

- Developing & Implementing Individualized Education Plans (IEPs)

- Providing Academic & Behavioral Support

- Advocating for Inclusive Policies & Rights of Children with Disabilities

1 Foundations of Special Education

📌 Concept, Meaning, and Scope of Special Education

◆ Concept & Meaning:

Special Education refers to **specially designed instruction** that meets the unique needs of children with disabilities. It provides **individualized learning plans, adaptive teaching strategies, and assistive technologies** to ensure equal educational opportunities.

◆ Scope of Special Education:

☑ **Early Intervention Programs** – Identifying disabilities at an early stage and providing necessary support.
☑ **Inclusive Education** – Integrating children with special needs into mainstream classrooms with necessary accommodations.
☑ **Special Schools** – Institutions specifically designed for children with severe disabilities.
☑ **Assistive Technologies** – Tools like Braille, speech-to-text software, and AAC devices.
☑ **Vocational Training** – Preparing students for employment opportunities based on their abilities.

📝 **Example:** A child with visual impairment using Braille books and screen readers for studying.

📌 Historical Perspective of Special Education

◆ Global Developments:

- **1800s** – Emergence of the first schools for children with disabilities (e.g., schools for the blind and deaf).

- **1900s** – Special education laws introduced in developed countries.

- **1975 – Education for All Handicapped Children Act (USA)** ensured free and appropriate public education (FAPE).

- **2006 – United Nations Convention on the Rights of Persons with Disabilities (UNCRPD)** recognized inclusive education as a fundamental right.

◆ India's Progress:

- **1887:** First special school for the blind established in Amritsar.

- **1974:** Integrated Education for Disabled Children (IEDC) scheme launched.

- **1995:** Persons with Disabilities (PWD) Act passed.

- **2016:** Rights of Persons with Disabilities (RPWD) Act replaced the 1995 Act, broadening the scope of disabilities.

📊 Table: Key Milestones in Special Education in India

Year	Event
1887	First school for the blind in Amritsar
1974	IEDC Scheme launched
1995	Persons with Disabilities (PWD) Act passed
2016	RPWD Act expanded disability categories

📌 Difference between Special, Integrated & Inclusive Education

📊 Comparison Table:

Feature	Special Education	Integrated Education	Inclusive Education
Placement	Separate Schools	Regular Schools	Regular Schools
Teaching Method	Specialized	Regular (No major changes)	Adaptive & Flexible
Support	Full Support	Minimal Support	Maximum Support

📌 Responsibilities & Classroom Structure of a Special Educator

◆ Responsibilities:

☑ **Assessing Student Needs** – Conducting evaluations to identify strengths and weaknesses.
☑ **Developing Individualized Education Plans (IEPs)** – Creating personalized goals for students.
☑ **Collaborating with General Educators** – Ensuring modifications in teaching methods.
☑ **Implementing Behavioral Interventions** – Managing classroom behavior effectively.
☑ **Providing Emotional & Social Support** – Encouraging self-confidence and social skills.

📊 **Table: Responsibilities of a Special Educator**

Responsibility	Description
Assessment	Identifying student strengths & needs
IEP Development	Creating personalized learning plans
Collaboration	Working with teachers & parents
Intervention	Implementing behavior & learning strategies

📌 Practice MCQs & PYQs

📚 MCQs:

1 Which law in India expanded the definition of disabilities in 2016? a) PWD Act 1995
b) RPWD Act 2016
c) RTE Act 2009
d) UNCRPD 2006
☑ **Answer:** (b) RPWD Act 2016

2 What does LRE (Least Restrictive Environment) mean? a) Placing all students in special schools
b) Providing maximum independence to students
c) Teaching students without any special support
d) Restricting students from mainstream education
☑ **Answer:** (b) Providing maximum independence to students

- **(DSSSB 2019)**: Which of the following is a primary objective of special education?
  a) Isolate students with disabilities
  b) Provide equal learning opportunities
  c) Follow a rigid curriculum
  d) Promote uniform learning methods
  ☑ **Answer:** (b) Provide equal learning opportunities

---

2 Understanding Disabilities & Their Classification

Definition & Classification of Disabilities (As per RPWD Act, 2016) 📜

The **Rights of Persons with Disabilities (RPWD) Act, 2016** recognizes **21 types of disabilities**, classifying them under broad categories. This classification plays a vital role in policy-making, educational planning, and ensuring necessary accommodations for individuals with disabilities.

21 Types of Disabilities (RPWD Act, 2016)

Here is a structured table listing the **21 disabilities** recognized under the **Rights of Persons with Disabilities (RPWD) Act, 2016**, along with brief details for each:

S.No	Disability	Description
1	**Blindness** 👁	Complete vision loss or visual acuity **<3/60**.
2	**Low Vision** 	Partial vision loss; can use **assistive devices**.

3	**Leprosy Cured Persons**	Cured but may have **residual deformities** or disabilities.
4	**Hearing Impairment (Deafness)**	Hearing loss of **70 dB or more** in both ears.
5	**Hard of Hearing**	Partial hearing loss (**60–70 dB**); may use **hearing aids**.
6	**Locomotor Disability**	Restriction of **limb movement** due to injury/disease.
7	**Dwarfism**	Adult height below **4'10"** due to genetic/medical reasons.
8	**Intellectual Disability**	Below-average intellectual functioning (**IQ < 70**).
9	**Mental Illness**	**Psychiatric conditions** affecting daily functioning.
10	**Autism Spectrum Disorder (ASD)**	Neurodevelopmental disorder affecting **communication/social skills**.
11	**Cerebral Palsy**	Neurological disorder affecting **muscle coordination**.
12	**Muscular Dystrophy**	Genetic disorder causing **muscle weakness** over time.
13	**Chronic Neurological Conditions**	Long-term **brain/spinal cord disorders** like epilepsy.
14	**Specific Learning Disabilities**	Disorders like **dyslexia**, affecting reading/writing.
15	**Multiple Sclerosis**	Autoimmune disease affecting the **nervous system**.
16	**Speech and Language Disability**	Difficulty in **speech production/comprehension**.
17	**Thalassemia**	**Genetic blood disorder** affecting hemoglobin production.
18	**Hemophilia**	**Blood clotting disorder** leading to excessive bleeding.
19	**Sickle Cell Disease**	**Genetic disorder** affecting red blood cells.

| 20 | **Multiple Disabilities** | **Combination** of two or more disabilities. |

| 21 | **Acid Attack Victims** 🔥 | Physical impairments due to **acid burns**. |

1 👤 Blindness – A Deep Dive! 👁

🔍 What is Blindness?

Blindness refers to a **complete or significant loss of vision** that **cannot** be corrected with glasses, lenses, or surgery. A person with blindness **struggles to see shapes, light, or any objects clearly**.

📜 Definition as per RPWD Act, 2016:

- **Visual acuity** less than **3/60** in the better eye with best correction.
- **Field of vision** restricted to **less than 10 degrees**.

⚠ What Causes Blindness?

Blindness can be **congenital** (from birth) or **acquired** due to various factors:

- 🧬 **Genetic conditions** (e.g., Retinitis Pigmentosa)
- 🏥 **Diseases** (e.g., Cataracts, Glaucoma, Diabetes-related blindness)
- 🙁 **Injuries** (e.g., Accidents, Chemical burns)
- 🦠 **Infections** (e.g., Trachoma, Vitamin A Deficiency)

⚫ How Does It Affect Life?

- **Education:** Difficulty reading textbooks, writing, and taking exams 📚✏
- **Employment:** Limited job opportunities in some fields 💼
- **Mobility:** Challenges in independent movement 🏃
- **Social Interaction:** Communication barriers in a visual world 👥

🔧 Assistive Devices & Technologies

Modern technology has empowered visually impaired individuals with **amazing tools**:

- 📖 **Braille System:** A tactile reading and writing system.
- 🎧 **Screen Readers:** Software like JAWS and NVDA that convert text to speech.
- 📏 **Smart Canes:** Canes with ultrasonic sensors to detect obstacles.
- 📱 **Voice Assistants & AI Apps:** Google Assistant, Seeing AI, Be My Eyes.

🎯 Government Support & Benefits

The **Indian Government** provides multiple benefits for visually impaired individuals:

- 🏛️ **Education & Job Reservations** under the RPWD Act.
- 💊 **Disability Pension & Financial Aid** to support independent living.
- 🏥 **Free Medical Treatment & Rehabilitation Programs.**

💡 **Fun Fact:** Louis Braille, who invented the Braille system, became blind at the age of **three** but transformed millions of lives with his invention! 🎉

2 🔍 Low Vision – A Closer Look! 👓

📌 What is Low Vision?

Low Vision is a condition where a person has **partial vision loss** that **cannot** be fully corrected with glasses, lenses, or surgery, but they can still use **assistive devices** to enhance their vision.

📜 Definition as per RPWD Act, 2016:

- **Visual acuity** between **3/60 and 6/18** in the better eye with best correction.
- **Significant reduction in the field of vision** but not total blindness.

⚠️ What Causes Low Vision?

- 🏥 **Diseases**: Glaucoma, Cataracts, Diabetic Retinopathy.
- 🧬 **Genetic Disorders**: Albinism, Retinitis Pigmentosa.
- 🙁 **Injuries**: Damage to the eye or optic nerve.
- 🦠 **Infections**: Corneal ulcers or severe eye infections.

⚫ How Does It Affect Life?

- **Reading & Writing**: Difficulty in recognizing small text and fine details.
- **Mobility**: Struggles with depth perception and identifying obstacles.
- **Daily Tasks**: Challenges in cooking, identifying faces, and using digital screens.

🛠️ Assistive Devices & Technologies

- 🔍 **Magnifiers**: Handheld or electronic devices for enlarging text.
- 🖥️ **Screen Magnification Software**: ZoomText, Windows Magnifier.
- ⚙️ **High-Contrast & Large-Print Books**: Makes reading easier.
- 🕶️ **Smart Glasses & AI-based Apps**: Envision AI, OrCam MyEye.

🎯 **Government Support & Benefits**

- 📚 **Educational Assistance**: Special study materials, digital learning tools.
- 🖼 **Job Reservations & Employment Aid**.
- 👤 **Medical Assistance & Financial Aid** for assistive devices.

💡 **Did You Know?** Helen Keller, one of the most famous advocates for the blind and visually impaired, had both **low vision and hearing loss** but still became an **author, activist, and educator!** 🎇

3 Leprosy Cured Persons 🩺

🔍 **What is Leprosy?**

Leprosy (Hansen's Disease) is a **chronic bacterial infection** caused by *Mycobacterium leprae*, affecting the **skin, nerves, and muscles**. If left untreated, it can lead to **permanent disabilities** like muscle weakness, loss of sensation, and deformities.

📜 **Who are Leprosy Cured Persons (LCP) as per RPWD Act, 2016?**

The RPWD Act recognizes **Leprosy Cured Persons** as individuals who:

1. Have **been cured** of leprosy but still face **physical deformities or disabilities**.

2. May experience **loss of sensation in hands/feet, weakness in limbs**, or **ulcers**.

3. Face **social stigma and discrimination**, affecting their quality of life.

⚠️ **Causes of Leprosy**

- 🦠 **Bacteria:** *Mycobacterium leprae* spreads through prolonged close contact.

- 🏠 **Poor Hygiene & Overcrowding:** Increases the risk of infection.

- 😷 **Weak Immune System:** Makes individuals more vulnerable.

⚫ **Impact on Life**

- **Physical Challenges:** Weakness in limbs, clawed fingers, foot drop, and ulcers.

- **Social Stigma:** Often isolated or discriminated against in society.

- **Employment Issues:** Limited job opportunities due to misconceptions.

- **Psychological Effects:** Anxiety, depression, and low self-esteem.

🛠 Assistive Devices & Rehabilitation

- ☐ **Physiotherapy & Surgery:** Helps in muscle strengthening and correcting deformities.

- 👟 **Special Footwear & Prosthetics:** Prevents ulcers and supports mobility.

- ✋ **Sensory Training:** Helps in improving the use of hands.

- 🤍 **Social Inclusion Programs:** Support groups and vocational training.

⊚ Government Support & Benefits

- 👛 **Financial Aid & Pension Schemes** for rehabilitation.

- 🏥 **Free Treatment & Healthcare Services** at government hospitals.

- 🏢 **Job Reservations & Employment Opportunities** under RPWD Act.

- 🏠 **Leprosy Rehabilitation Homes** for affected individuals.

💡 Did You Know?

India accounts for **over 50% of global leprosy cases**, but **early treatment with Multi-Drug Therapy (MDT)** can **completely cure the disease** and prevent disabilities! ⚫

4 Hearing Impairment (Deafness) 🔊

🔍 What is Hearing Impairment?

Hearing Impairment refers to **partial or complete loss of hearing** in one or both ears, affecting a person's ability to hear sounds clearly. It can range from **mild hearing loss** to **total deafness**.

📑 Definition as per RPWD Act, 2016

- **Hearing Impairment (Deafness):** A **70 dB or more** hearing loss in both ears.

- **Hard of Hearing:** A **60-70 dB** hearing loss, where a person can still hear with hearing aids.

⚠ Causes of Hearing Impairment

- 🧬 **Genetic Factors:** Inherited hearing loss.

- 🤰 **Birth Complications:** Premature birth, infections during pregnancy.

- 🔊 **Loud Noise Exposure:** Constant exposure to high-decibel sounds (machines, music, fireworks).

- 🦠 **Ear Infections & Diseases:** Meningitis, Otitis Media, Mumps, Measles.

- 💊 **Ototoxic Medications:** Certain antibiotics and chemotherapy drugs.

- ☹ **Head or Ear Injuries:** Trauma affecting the auditory system.

⚫ Impact on Life

- **Communication Barriers:** Difficulty in understanding speech, especially in noisy environments.

- **Education Challenges:** Delayed speech and language development in children.

- **Social & Emotional Effects:** Isolation, frustration, and difficulty in socializing.

- **Employment Issues:** Limited career opportunities in fields requiring verbal communication.

🛠 Assistive Devices & Technologies

- 🎧 **Hearing Aids:** Small electronic devices that amplify sound.

- 👂 **Cochlear Implants:** Surgically implanted devices for profound hearing loss.

- ✋ **Sign Language:** Visual communication using hand gestures and facial expressions.

- ✏ **Speech-to-Text Apps:** AI-powered apps that convert speech into text (e.g., Ava, Otter.ai).

- 📺 **Captioning & Subtitles:** Helps in understanding conversations on TV and online videos.

◎ **Government Support & Benefits**

- 🏫 **Special Education Programs:** Schools for children with hearing impairments.

- ▦ **Job Reservations & Skill Training** for employment opportunities.

- ⚱ **Financial Aid for Assistive Devices:** Subsidized hearing aids and cochlear implants.

- ▦ **Free Medical Treatment & Speech Therapy:** Available under government health schemes.

💡 **Did You Know?**
The **first Indian sign language dictionary** was launched in **2018** to promote communication accessibility for the **hearing impaired community!** 📚✋

5 Hard of Hearing 🎧

🔍 **What is Hard of Hearing?**

"Hard of Hearing" refers to **partial hearing loss** where a person has difficulty hearing **but is not completely deaf**. Unlike total deafness, individuals with this condition can benefit from **hearing aids, cochlear implants, and assistive devices** to improve communication.

📜 **Definition as per RPWD Act, 2016**

- A person with **hearing loss between 60–70 dB** in both ears.

- Unlike complete deafness (**70 dB or more**), some hearing ability remains.

- May struggle with **understanding speech, especially in noisy environments**.

⚠ **Causes of Hard of Hearing**

- 🧬 **Genetic Causes:** Family history of hearing loss.

- 👶 **Prenatal & Birth Issues:** Infections during pregnancy (e.g., rubella), low birth weight.

- 🔊 **Loud Noise Exposure:** Prolonged exposure to **loud music, industrial noise, or explosions**.

- 💊 **Ear Infections & Diseases:** Chronic ear infections, Meniere's disease, or fluid buildup.

     https://www.specialeducationnotes.in

- 🏷️ **Ototoxic Drugs:** Certain antibiotics, chemotherapy drugs, or high doses of aspirin.

- 🙁 **Head or Ear Trauma:** Injuries damaging the auditory system.

🔘 Impact on Life

- **Speech & Communication Issues:** Difficulty in understanding words, especially in noisy areas.

- **Educational Challenges:** Struggles with classroom learning due to unclear hearing.

- **Social Barriers:** Difficulty in conversations, leading to **isolation or frustration**.

- **Employment Issues:** Challenges in jobs requiring frequent verbal communication.

🛠️ Assistive Devices & Rehabilitation

- 🎧 **Hearing Aids:** Devices that amplify sound, making it easier to hear.

- 🦻 **Cochlear Implants:** For those with severe hearing loss.

- 🎙️ **Assistive Listening Devices (ALDs):** Helps in **reducing background noise**.

- 📱 **Speech-to-Text Apps:** Convert spoken words into written text for better communication.

- ✋ **Lip Reading & Sign Language Training:** Helps in better understanding conversations.

⏺️ Government Support & Benefits

- 🏫 **Special Education Support:** Schools with audio enhancement systems.

- 🎛️ **Job Reservations & Skill Training** under RPWD Act.

- 🏺 **Financial Assistance for Hearing Aids & Implants.**

- 🏥 **Free or Subsidized Medical Treatment & Speech Therapy.**

💡 **Did You Know?**
The world's first **hearing aid** was invented in the **17th century** and was shaped like a **large ear trumpet!** 🎙️🦻

6 Locomotor Disability – Movement Matters!

Imagine This:

A child wants to play with friends, but their legs don't support them. A worker loses mobility after an accident. A student struggles to reach class due to a lack of ramps. **This is what locomotor disability feels like.**

Let's break it down in an **interesting** and **exam-friendly** way!

What is Locomotor Disability?

Loss or limitation of movement due to problems in bones, muscles, or nerves.
Affects arms, legs, spine, or the entire body.
Can be **from birth** (congenital) or **acquired** due to accident or disease.

Defined in RPWD Act, 2016: "A person who has **restricted movement** due to dysfunction of bones, joints, or muscles."

Why Does It Happen? (Causes)

◆ **Birth Defects:** Clubfoot, brittle bones
◆ **Infections & Diseases:** Polio, Cerebral Palsy, Muscular Dystrophy
◆ **Nerve Disorders:** Stroke, Spinal Cord Injury, Multiple Sclerosis
◆ **Accidents & Amputations:** Road accidents, work injuries
◆ **Arthritis & Ageing Issues:** Weak joints, osteoporosis

How Does It Affect Life?

Limited Mobility: Walking, standing, or using stairs becomes tough.
Education Barriers: Need for ramps, adapted seating, and digital tools.
Employment Struggles: Many jobs require movement; need for inclusivity.
Social Challenges: Dependence on others for movement, accessibility issues.

😟 **Real-life Impact?** Imagine wanting to go to school or work, but **no wheelchair ramps** exist. **That's a real problem!**

🛠 How Can Technology Help?

◆ **Prosthetic Limbs:** Artificial legs & hands for amputees 🦿
◆ **Smart Wheelchairs:** Electric & AI-driven for easy movement ♿
◆ **Exoskeletons:** Robotic suits to help paralyzed people walk 🤖
◆ **Voice-Control Devices:** Computers and gadgets controlled by speech 🎙
◆ **Physiotherapy & Exercises:** Strength-building workouts for recovery 🏋

🎯 What is the Government Doing?

🏛 **Sugamya Bharat Abhiyan (Accessible India Campaign):** Making places wheelchair-friendly!

💼 **Job Reservations:** Quotas for disabled persons in government jobs.
🚗 **Transport Concessions:** Discounts on trains, buses, flights.
💰 **Financial Aid:** Scholarships, pensions, and free assistive devices.
🏥 **Medical Benefits:** Free surgeries, therapy, and mobility aids.

🔥 Inspiring Story

Meet Arunima Sinha – The First Female Amputee to Climb Mount Everest! 🏔
She lost her leg in an accident but didn't give up. With a prosthetic limb, **she climbed the world's highest peak!** 💥

💡 **Moral:** Locomotor disability may slow someone down, but it **cannot stop** them!

✏ Your Turn:
Kya tumhe koi aisa person ya technology pata hai jo locomotor disability walon ki help karti ho? 🤔

---

                    https://www.specialeducationnotes.in

🚀 **Final Thought:**

Mobility is **freedom**. Accessible places, advanced technology, and social inclusion can make life easier for people with locomotor disabilities!

7 ✎ Dwarfism – Small Height, Big Achievements! 💪

✨ Imagine This:

A child walks into a toy store, and the cashier mistakes them for a toddler—**but they're actually 18 years old.** A talented engineer struggles at work because the office furniture is too high. A student can't reach the blackboard in class. **This is what life can be like for someone with dwarfism.**

Let's **dive in** and make this topic **interesting, relatable, and exam-ready!** 🚀

😊 What is Dwarfism?

Dwarfism is a **medical condition where a person's height remains significantly shorter than average due to genetic or medical reasons.**

📌 **Definition as per RPWD Act, 2016:**

- An **adult height of 4 feet 10 inches (147 cm) or less.**

- Caused by **abnormal bone growth** or **hormonal issues.**

❓ Why Does It Happen? (Causes)

◆ **Genetic Mutations:** Achondroplasia (most common form of dwarfism) 🍬
◆ **Hormonal Deficiency:** Growth hormone issues during childhood 📉
◆ **Bone Disorders:** Brittle bones, skeletal dysplasia 🦴
◆ **Malnutrition:** Lack of essential nutrients during early growth 🥔
◆ **Medical Conditions:** Turner Syndrome, Hypothyroidism 🩺

🌑 How Does It Affect Life?

🗄 **Education:** Difficulty using regular desks and reaching the blackboard.
💼 **Employment Challenges:** Workspaces and uniforms not designed for them.
🏠 **Daily Life Struggles:** High shelves, ATMs, and transportation pose issues.
🔘 **Social Stigma:** People often treat them like children or underestimate their abilities.
⚕ **Health Risks:** Joint pain, breathing difficulties, spinal curvature.

😟 **Real-life Struggle?** Imagine walking into a room where every chair, table, and shelf is built **for giants.**

🛠 How Can Technology & Innovation Help?

◆ **Adaptive Furniture & Vehicles:** Lower countertops, adjustable chairs, modified cars 🚗
◆ **Growth Hormone Therapy:** Helps some cases if detected early 💉
◆ **Custom Prosthetics & Orthopedic Support:** Special shoes, braces 👟
◆ **Voice-Controlled Devices:** AI-based gadgets to reduce physical effort 🎙
◆ **Awareness Campaigns:** Fighting misconceptions & promoting inclusivity 🗣

🎯 What is the Government Doing?

🏫 **Education Rights:** Schools must provide **low-height seating & accessible learning spaces**.
💼 **Job Reservations & Skill Training:** Employment opportunities in government & private sectors.
🚗 **Transport Benefits:** Custom seating and travel concessions in public transport.
💰 **Financial Aid:** Disability pensions & healthcare benefits.
🏥 **Medical Support:** Free or subsidized treatment for growth-related conditions.

🔥 Inspiring Story – Never Let Height Define You!

🎤 **Meet Jyoti Amge – The World's Shortest Woman!** 🌍🏆

- Born with dwarfism, **Jyoti stands at just 2 feet 1 inch (63 cm).**
- She became a **Bollywood actress & motivational speaker**.
- Holds a **Guinness World Record** and promotes awareness about dwarfism!

💡 **Lesson:** Height doesn't decide success—**your mindset does!** 🚀

😕 Let's Think!

How can schools, offices, and public places be **more inclusive** for people with dwarfism? 🏫 💼 🚗

🚀 Final Thought:

👉 **Dwarfism is not a limitation—it's just a different way of experiencing the world.**
👉 With **accessible design, inclusivity, and social awareness**, we can create a world where height is never a barrier!

8 🧠 Intellectual Disability – Understanding Cognitive Challenges

📌 What is Intellectual Disability?

Intellectual Disability (ID) is a condition where a person has **limitations in intellectual functioning (IQ below 70) and adaptive behavior**, affecting their ability to learn, reason, and perform everyday tasks. It develops **before the age of 18** and impacts education, employment, and social life.

📜 **Definition as per RPWD Act, 2016**

A condition characterized by **significant limitations in intellectual functioning** (reasoning, problem-solving) and **adaptive behavior** (communication, social skills, and self-care).

😊 Causes of Intellectual Disability

1. **Genetic Disorders** – Down Syndrome, Fragile X Syndrome 🧬

2. **Birth-related Issues** – Premature birth, oxygen deprivation at birth 👶

3. **Nutritional Deficiencies** – Iodine deficiency, malnutrition 🍽️

4. **Brain Infections & Injuries** – Meningitis, head trauma 😕

5. **Environmental Factors** – Exposure to toxins (lead, alcohol, drugs) ☠️

⬤ How Does It Affect Life?

☑️ **Learning Challenges** – Difficulty understanding concepts and remembering things.
☑️ **Social & Communication Barriers** – Trouble making friends, expressing emotions.
☑️ **Employment Struggles** – Need for supportive work environments.
☑️ **Daily Living Skills** – Dependence on caregivers for basic tasks like cooking or money management.

💡 **Real-life Scenario:** Imagine a student who wants to answer a simple math question but struggles to process numbers. This is a daily challenge for someone with ID.

🛠️ Supportive Technologies & Therapies

◆ **Special Education Programs** – Individualized learning strategies.
◆ **Speech & Occupational Therapy** – Helps with communication and life skills.
◆ **Assistive Apps & Tools** – Text-to-speech software, visual learning aids.
◆ **Vocational Training** – Skill-building programs for employment.

◎ Government Support & Benefits

🏛️ **Inclusive Education** – Special schools & reserved seats in regular schools.
💼 **Job Reservations & Self-employment Support** – Special quotas in government jobs.
⏳ **Financial Aid & Disability Pension** – Monthly allowances for independent living.
🏥 **Healthcare Benefits** – Free therapy, counseling, and medical treatment.

🔥 Inspiring Story – A Genius Beyond Limits!

💡 **Stephen Wiltshire, a man with an intellectual disability, became a world-famous artist** 🖼️ 🎨.

He has **autistic savant syndrome**, allowing him to draw entire cityscapes from memory after just one look!

🚀 Final Thought:

Intellectual Disability is not the end—it's just a different way of learning and living! With the right support, individuals can lead **independent, successful lives**.

9 ⬤ Mental Illness – The Invisible Battle

📌 What is Mental Illness?

Mental illness refers to **disorders that affect a person's thinking, mood, behavior, or emotions**, making daily life challenging. These conditions can be **temporary or lifelong** and range from mild to severe.

📜 Definition as per RPWD Act, 2016

A substantial disorder of thinking, mood, perception, orientation, or memory that severely **impairs judgment, behavior, or daily functioning. (Excludes intellectual disabilities.)**

😊 Common Types of Mental Illness

◆ **Depression** – Persistent sadness, loss of interest in activities.
◆ **Anxiety Disorders** – Excessive fear, worry, or panic attacks.
◆ **Bipolar Disorder** – Extreme mood swings between highs (mania) and lows (depression).
◆ **Schizophrenia** – Hallucinations, delusions, and disorganized thinking.
◆ **Obsessive-Compulsive Disorder (OCD)** – Repetitive thoughts and behaviors.
◆ **Post-Traumatic Stress Disorder (PTSD)** – Stress after a traumatic event.

⬤ How Does It Affect Life?

☑ **Difficulty in Education & Work** – Trouble concentrating or maintaining routine.
☑ **Strained Relationships** – Social withdrawal, lack of communication.
☑ **Emotional Distress** – Constant worry, fear, or sadness.
☑ **Physical Impact** – Insomnia, weight changes, and fatigue.

💡 **Real-life Scenario:** A student with severe anxiety wants to speak in class but feels paralyzed with fear. This is a daily struggle for many!

✄ Supportive Therapies & Treatments

◆ **Psychotherapy (Counseling)** – Talking with a professional helps in managing emotions.
◆ **Medication** – Antidepressants, mood stabilizers, or anti-anxiety drugs.
◆ **Mindfulness & Relaxation Techniques** – Yoga, meditation, breathing exercises.
◆ **Support Groups** – Peer support to share experiences and coping strategies.

◎ Government Support & Benefits

🖼 **Free Treatment & Counseling Centers** – Available under National Mental Health Programme.
📚 **Inclusive Education** – Special provisions in schools and colleges.
💼 **Employment Support** – Job reservations and workplace mental health policies.
🏅 **Disability Pension & Financial Aid** – Government schemes for treatment and rehabilitation.

⛱ Inspiring Story – Strength Over Stigma!

✏ **Deepika Padukone, one of India's top actresses, battled depression but spoke openly about it.** She started the **Live Love Laugh Foundation** to help others facing mental health issues!

---

     https://www.specialeducationnotes.in

🚀 Final Thought:

Mental Illness is NOT a weakness! With **proper care, support, and awareness,** people can lead **happy and productive lives.**

🔟 🧩 Autism Spectrum Disorder (ASD) – A Unique Way of Experiencing the World

📌 What is Autism Spectrum Disorder?

Autism Spectrum Disorder (ASD) is a neurodevelopmental condition that affects a person's ability to communicate, interact socially, and process sensory information. Since autism exists on a spectrum, its impact varies from mild to severe.

📜 **Definition as per RPWD Act, 2016**

A condition marked by challenges in social communication, restricted interests, and repetitive behaviors, significantly affecting daily life.

🧐 What Makes Autism Unique?

✅ **Different Ways of Thinking – Logical and detail-oriented, but struggle with abstract concepts.**
✅ **Sensory Sensitivities – Some may be hypersensitive to light, sounds, or textures, while others may seek strong sensations.**
✅ **Special Interests – Intense focus on specific topics like math, music, or trains.**
✅ **Difficulty Understanding Social Cues – Struggles with facial expressions, sarcasm, or indirect communication.**
✅ **Strong Routines & Repetition – Prefers predictable environments; changes can cause distress.**

💡 **Did You Know? Many individuals with autism have exceptional talents in memory, art, music, and pattern recognition!**

🚦 Early Signs of Autism (Not the Same for Everyone!)

👶 In Infants & Toddlers

- **No eye contact or response to their name.**

- Delayed speech or unusual speech patterns (e.g., echolalia – repeating words).

- Repetitive movements (hand flapping, rocking).

In School-Aged Children

- Difficulty making friends or preferring to be alone.

- Deep interest in one topic, like maps or numbers.

- Struggles with changes in routine.

In Adults

- Social anxiety, difficulty understanding others' emotions.

- Exceptional problem-solving abilities but challenges in teamwork.

- Preference for structured, predictable tasks.

How Does Autism Affect Life?

Education Challenges & Strengths – Some struggle with traditional learning, while others excel in specific subjects.
Employment Struggles & Opportunities – Difficulty in workplace communication but great at structured tasks.
Daily Life Adaptations – Sensory-friendly environments help them thrive.
Family & Social Life – Need patient and understanding relationships.

Real-life Impact: Imagine being in a classroom where the ceiling fan's noise feels as loud as a fire alarm—this is how sensory overload feels for some autistic individuals.

How Can We Support People with Autism?

◆ Structured Learning Approaches – Visual schedules, step-by-step instructions.
◆ Speech & Social Skills Therapy – Helps in improving communication.
◆ Occupational Therapy – Supports motor skills and sensory challenges.

◆ **Assistive Technology** – Apps for communication, noise-canceling headphones.
◆ **Inclusive Work & School Policies** – Specialized programs for employment and education.

🎯 Government Support & Benefits

🏫 **Special Education Programs** – Individualized Education Plans (IEPs) in schools.
💼 **Employment Support** – Skill-based training for job placements.
⏱️ **Financial Assistance** – Disability pensions & therapy funding.
🏥 **Healthcare Benefits** – Free/subsidized therapies & interventions.

🔥 Inspiring Story – Seeing the World Differently!

❄️ Temple Grandin – Diagnosed with autism, she struggled with social skills but became a world-famous scientist & animal behavior expert. Her innovative designs revolutionized the cattle industry!

🚀 Final Thought:

Autism is not a disability; it's a different ability! With the right support, understanding, and acceptance, autistic individuals can achieve extraordinary things.

1️⃣1️⃣ Cerebral Palsy – Challenges in Movement & Coordination

📌 What is Cerebral Palsy?

Cerebral Palsy (CP) is a **neurological disorder** that affects **muscle movement, coordination, and posture**. It occurs due to **brain damage before, during, or shortly after birth**. The severity varies—some individuals have **mild movement difficulties**, while others may need lifelong assistance.

📜 Definition as per RPWD Act, 2016

A **group of movement disorders** caused by **non-progressive brain damage**, affecting **muscle tone, posture, and motor skills**.

🛏 Causes of Cerebral Palsy

🩺 **Birth complications** – Lack of oxygen during birth.
💊 **Infections during pregnancy** – Rubella, cytomegalovirus.
😞 **Head injuries** – Trauma before or after birth.
🧬 **Genetic mutations** – Rare but possible cause.

🔍 Types of Cerebral Palsy

⬡ **Spastic CP** – Stiff, tight muscles causing jerky movements (most common).
🔄 **Dyskinetic CP** – Involuntary, uncontrolled movements.
⚖ **Ataxic CP** – Poor balance and coordination.
🔄 **Mixed CP** – Combination of two or more types.

⬤ How Does It Affect Life?

☑ **Difficulty Walking** – May require crutches, braces, or wheelchairs.
☑ **Speech Challenges** – Trouble in pronunciation and expression.
☑ **Fine Motor Skill Issues** – Difficulty holding objects, using buttons, or writing.
☑ **Associated Conditions** – Some may have seizures, vision/hearing issues, or learning disabilities.

💡 **Example:** A child with CP may struggle to hold a spoon or walk steadily but can have a sharp memory and creativity.

✄ Supportive Therapies & Treatments

◆ **Physical Therapy** – Improves mobility and posture.
◆ **Speech Therapy** – Helps with communication and swallowing.
◆ **Occupational Therapy** – Develops daily life skills.
◆ **Assistive Devices** – Braces, wheelchairs, and voice-assisted technology.
◆ **Medications & Surgery** – To reduce muscle stiffness and improve movement.

🎯 Government Support & Benefits

🏫 **Inclusive Education** – Special schools and assistive learning programs.
💼 **Employment Opportunities** – Skill development for independent work.

Financial Aid & Pension – Support for therapy and assistive devices.
Healthcare Schemes – Free treatment under government programs.

Inspiring Story – A Champion Beyond Limits!

Dr. Satendra Singh, a doctor with cerebral palsy, fought for disability rights and improved accessibility in India's medical institutions.

Final Thought:

Cerebral Palsy **doesn't define a person's potential**. With **therapy, technology, and acceptance**, individuals with CP can live **independent and fulfilling lives**.

1 2 Muscular Dystrophy – Progressive Muscle Weakness

What is Muscular Dystrophy?

Muscular Dystrophy (MD) is a **group of genetic disorders** that cause **gradual muscle weakening and loss of muscle mass**. Over time, affected muscles become **weak and less functional**, making movements like walking, sitting, and even breathing difficult.

Definition as per RPWD Act, 2016

A **group of inherited disorders** characterized by **progressive degeneration and weakness of skeletal muscles**.

Causes & Risk Factors

Genetic Mutations – Errors in genes responsible for muscle structure.
Family History – Inherited from parents in most cases.
Progressive in Nature – Symptoms worsen over time, leading to severe disability.

Types of Muscular Dystrophy

1. **Duchenne MD (DMD)** – Most common in children, affects boys more than girls.
2. **Becker MD (BMD)** – Milder than Duchenne but progresses over time.
3. **Limb-Girdle MD** – Affects shoulder and hip muscles first.

4 **Facioscapulohumeral MD (FSHD)** – Weakness in facial, shoulder, and upper arm muscles.
5 **Myotonic Dystrophy** – Muscle stiffness along with weakness.

🔘 How Does It Affect Life?

☑ **Loss of Mobility** – Walking becomes difficult; some may need wheelchairs.
☑ **Breathing & Heart Problems** – In severe cases, muscles supporting breathing and heart function weaken.
☑ **Difficulty in Everyday Tasks** – Holding objects, climbing stairs, or even chewing food can be challenging.
☑ **Shortened Lifespan (in severe cases)** – Some types, like Duchenne MD, reduce life expectancy due to heart and lung complications.

💡 **Example:** A child with Duchenne MD may be able to walk normally at first but could need a wheelchair by their teenage years.

✂ Supportive Therapies & Treatments

◆ **Physical Therapy** – Keeps muscles flexible and delays stiffness.
◆ **Braces & Mobility Aids** – Supports weak muscles and improves movement.
◆ **Respiratory Support** – Breathing exercises or ventilators in severe cases.
◆ **Speech Therapy** – Helps in cases where facial muscles are affected.
◆ **Gene Therapy (Future Hope)** – Ongoing research aims to repair faulty genes.

🎯 Government Support & Benefits

📋 **Educational Inclusion** – Special assistance in schools.
💼 **Job Reservations & Skill Training** – Programs to provide employment opportunities.
🧴 **Disability Pension & Financial Aid** – Support for medical care and assistive devices.
🏥 **Free Treatment under Government Schemes** – Subsidized therapy and medical care.

🔥 Inspiring Story – Strength in Adversity!

✷ **Stephen Hawking**, though not diagnosed with muscular dystrophy but with a progressive neurological disorder, defied all odds and became one of the world's most brilliant physicists. His story inspires millions battling degenerative diseases.

🚀 Final Thought:

Muscular Dystrophy is **challenging, but medical advancements and assistive technologies** are improving the quality of life for affected individuals. **Early intervention, proper care, and strong support systems** can help them lead fulfilling lives.

1️⃣ 3️⃣ Chronic Neurological Conditions – Long-Term Disorders of the Nervous System

📌 What Are Chronic Neurological Conditions?

These are **long-lasting disorders** that affect the **brain, spinal cord, or nerves**, leading to difficulties in **movement, sensation, cognition, or other body functions**. These conditions can be **progressive, recurrent, or permanent**.

📜 **Definition as per RPWD Act, 2016**

A group of **neurological disorders** that persist over time, significantly impacting a person's **daily life, independence, and well-being**.

🪨 Common Causes & Risk Factors

⚪ **Genetic Factors** – Some conditions, like epilepsy or Huntington's disease, are inherited.
⏳ **Aging** – Neurological disorders like Parkinson's disease are more common in older adults.
🙁 **Injuries & Strokes** – Trauma to the brain or spine can lead to permanent nerve damage.
🦠 **Infections & Autoimmune Disorders** – Conditions like Multiple Sclerosis occur when the immune system attacks nerves.
☢️ **Toxins & Environmental Factors** – Exposure to harmful chemicals may trigger conditions like neuropathy.

🔍 Examples of Chronic Neurological Conditions

1 **Epilepsy** – Sudden, recurring seizures due to abnormal brain activity.
2 **Parkinson's Disease** – A movement disorder causing tremors, stiffness, and slow movement.
3 **Multiple Sclerosis (MS)** – The immune system attacks the nervous system, affecting movement and coordination.
4 **Alzheimer's & Dementia** – Progressive loss of memory and cognitive functions.
5 **Migraine & Chronic Headaches** – Severe, recurring headaches affecting daily life.

⚫ How Do These Conditions Affect Life?

☑ **Physical Limitations** – Muscle weakness, tremors, difficulty in walking.
☑ **Cognitive Challenges** – Memory loss, difficulty concentrating, confusion.
☑ **Speech & Communication Issues** – Some conditions affect the ability to speak clearly.
☑ **Emotional & Social Impact** – Anxiety, depression, and isolation due to long-term illness.
☑ **Dependency on Caregivers** – In severe cases, individuals may require lifelong support.

💡 **Example:** A person with **Parkinson's disease** may struggle to hold a cup steadily due to hand tremors but can still think and reason normally.

🛠 Treatment & Management

◆ **Medications** – Used to control symptoms (e.g., anti-seizure drugs for epilepsy).
◆ **Physical & Occupational Therapy** – Helps improve mobility and daily life skills.
◆ **Cognitive & Speech Therapy** – Supports those with memory or communication issues.
◆ **Assistive Devices** – Walking aids, communication apps, and brain stimulation therapies.
◆ **Lifestyle Modifications** – Proper diet, exercise, and stress management can slow disease progression.

🎯 Government Support & Benefits

🏥 **Free or Subsidized Medical Care** – Under disability welfare programs.
🎓 **Educational Assistance** – Special provisions for students with neurological disabilities.
💼 **Employment Benefits** – Reservation in government jobs and workplace accommodations.
⚖ **Disability Pension & Financial Aid** – Support for long-term care and treatments.

---

https://www.specialeducationnotes.in

🔥 Inspiring Story – Defying Neurological Challenges!

✳️ **Muhammad Ali**, the legendary boxer, battled **Parkinson's disease** but remained an inspiration in his fight against disability. He continued raising awareness and helping others despite his condition.

🚀 Final Thought:

Chronic Neurological Conditions **may not have a cure**, but with **early diagnosis, proper management, and strong support systems**, individuals can lead a **productive and meaningful life**.

1️⃣ 4️⃣ Specific Learning Disabilities – Hidden Challenges in Learning

📌 What Are Specific Learning Disabilities (SLDs)?

SLDs are **neurological disorders** that affect a person's ability to **read, write, spell, or do math**, despite having normal intelligence. These conditions make traditional learning difficult, requiring **special teaching methods** and **supportive tools**.

📜 Definition as per RPWD Act, 2016

A disorder that affects **one or more psychological processes related to understanding or using language, spoken or written**, impacting academic skills like reading, writing, and math.

🛡️ Causes & Risk Factors

🧠 **Brain Function Differences** – Structural or functional differences in the brain.
👶 **Premature Birth or Low Birth Weight** – May increase the risk of learning difficulties.
🧬 **Genetics** – A family history of learning disabilities can be a contributing factor.
🧪 **Prenatal Exposure to Toxins** – Alcohol, drugs, or infections during pregnancy may cause learning disorders.
🏠 **Environmental Factors** – Poor nutrition, lack of stimulation in early childhood.

🔍 Types of Specific Learning Disabilities

📖 **Dyslexia** – Difficulty in reading and recognizing words.
✏️ **Dysgraphia** – Trouble with handwriting and spelling.
🔢 **Dyscalculia** – Struggles with numbers and math concepts.
🧑‍🦯 **Auditory Processing Disorder** – Difficulty understanding spoken language.
👀 **Visual Processing Disorder** – Problems in interpreting visual information like shapes, letters, and patterns.

🔵 How Do SLDs Affect Life?

☑️ **Difficulty in Reading & Writing** – Slow reading speed, frequent spelling mistakes.
☑️ **Math Challenges** – Confusion with numbers, difficulty in calculations.
☑️ **Poor Memory & Organization** – Trouble remembering instructions or keeping track of assignments.
☑️ **Social & Emotional Struggles** – Low self-confidence, frustration, and anxiety about school.
☑️ **Delayed Academic Progress** – Despite normal intelligence, learning takes longer than peers.

💡 **Example:** A student with **dyslexia** may be highly intelligent but struggle to read even simple words, leading to frustration in school.

🛠️ Supportive Strategies & Interventions

◆ **Multisensory Learning Techniques** – Teaching through visuals, audio, and touch.
◆ **Assistive Technology** – Speech-to-text software, audiobooks, and special fonts.
◆ **Individualized Education Plans (IEPs)** – Special education programs tailored to student needs.
◆ **Extra Time & Alternative Assessments** – Adjustments in exams to support students with SLDs.
◆ **Parental & Teacher Training** – Awareness programs to help families and educators support children effectively.

🎯 Government Support & Benefits

📚 **Special Education Programs** – Free or subsidized education support for students with SLDs.
📝 **Exam Accommodations** – Extra time, scribes, and alternative question formats.
💼 **Employment Support** – Skill training programs for career success.
🏺 **Financial Assistance** – Grants and scholarships for children with learning disabilities.

🐣 Inspiring Story – Overcoming Dyslexia!

✳️ **Albert Einstein** had difficulties with reading and spelling as a child, but he went on to become one of the greatest scientists in history. His story proves that **learning disabilities do not limit intelligence or potential**.

🚀 Final Thought:

Specific Learning Disabilities **may make learning challenging**, but **early identification, right teaching methods, and proper support** can help individuals **achieve their full potential**.

1 5 Multiple Sclerosis – The Body Attacking Itself

📌 What is Multiple Sclerosis (MS)?

Multiple Sclerosis (MS) is a **chronic autoimmune disorder** where the body's **immune system mistakenly attacks the protective covering (myelin) of nerve fibers** in the brain and spinal cord. This leads to **communication problems between the brain and the rest of the body**, causing **muscle weakness, vision problems, and coordination issues**.

📜 **Definition as per RPWD Act, 2016**

A **progressive neurological disorder** that results in varying degrees of **physical and cognitive disabilities due to nerve damage**.

🪨 Causes & Risk Factors

🧫 **Autoimmune Disorder** – The body's defense system mistakenly attacks healthy nerve cells.
🧬 **Genetics** – A family history of MS may increase the risk.
🌐 **Environmental Factors** – Low vitamin D levels and viral infections (like Epstein-Barr virus) may trigger MS.
👩 **Gender Factor** – Women are **two to three times more likely** to develop MS than men.
⏳ **Age & Lifestyle** – Usually diagnosed between **20–40 years**; smoking can worsen symptoms.

🔎 Types of Multiple Sclerosis

1 Relapsing-Remitting MS (RRMS) – The most common type, involving flare-ups followed by recovery periods.
2 Primary Progressive MS (PPMS) – Gradual worsening of symptoms without relapses.
3 Secondary Progressive MS (SPMS) – Initially relapsing-remitting, but later becomes steadily progressive.
4 Progressive-Relapsing MS (PRMS) – Rare but severe, with no remission between flare-ups.

⚫ How Does MS Affect Life?

☑ **Muscle Weakness & Fatigue** – Difficulty walking or moving hands properly.
☑ **Balance & Coordination Issues** – Frequent falls or unsteady movements.
☑ **Vision Problems** – Blurred or double vision due to nerve damage.
☑ **Cognitive Impairment** – Trouble with memory, concentration, and problem-solving.
☑ **Speech & Swallowing Difficulties** – Slurred speech and trouble eating in later stages.
☑ **Bladder & Bowel Dysfunction** – Loss of control or frequent urges.

💡 **Example:** A person with MS may experience **normal days followed by sudden episodes of extreme weakness**, making daily life unpredictable.

🛠 Treatment & Management

◆ **Disease-Modifying Drugs (DMDs)** – Help slow down disease progression.
◆ **Physical Therapy** – Improves movement, flexibility, and muscle strength.
◆ **Speech & Cognitive Therapy** – Supports communication and memory functions.
◆ **Vitamin D & Healthy Diet** – Reduces inflammation and improves overall health.
◆ **Assistive Devices** – Walking aids, cooling vests (to manage heat sensitivity).

🎯 Government Support & Benefits

🏥 **Free or Subsidized Treatment** – MS patients can access financial aid for medicines and therapy.
💼 **Job Reservations & Workplace Adjustments** – Flexible work arrangements for MS patients.
📚 **Educational Assistance** – Special allowances in exams and learning accommodations.
⚖ **Disability Pension & Financial Support** – Monthly aid for those severely affected.

---

  https://www.specialeducationnotes.in

🔥 Inspiring Story – Fighting MS with Courage!

✳️ **Selma Blair**, a Hollywood actress, was diagnosed with MS but continued her career, raising awareness and inspiring millions to never give up.

🚀 Final Thought:

MS is a **lifelong condition**, but **early diagnosis, proper treatment, and strong support systems** can help individuals **manage symptoms and lead fulfilling lives**.

1 6 Speech and Language Disability

📌 What is Speech and Language Disability?

It is a condition where a person **struggles to speak clearly, understand language, or express thoughts effectively**. It can range from **mild difficulties in pronunciation to complete loss of speech**. These disabilities are **not linked to intelligence** but can significantly impact daily life, education, and social interactions.

📜 Definition as per RPWD Act, 2016

A **permanent disability** that affects an individual's ability to **communicate verbally**, caused by **neurological, developmental, or structural impairments**.

🪨 Causes & Risk Factors

👶 **Developmental Delays** – Some children take longer to develop speech skills.
🧠 **Brain Damage** – Stroke, head injuries, or cerebral palsy can cause speech impairments.
🦠 **Infections & Diseases** – Conditions like meningitis can affect speech centers in the brain.
👂 **Hearing Impairment** – Hearing loss can prevent proper speech development.
🧩 **Neurological Disorders** – Autism, Parkinson's disease, and multiple sclerosis can impact speech.

🔑 Types of Speech and Language Disabilities

🎤 **Dysarthria** – Weak muscles make speech slurred or slow.
🧩 **Apraxia of Speech** – Brain struggles to coordinate mouth movements for speech.
📢 **Stuttering (Stammering)** – Repetition of sounds or difficulty starting words.

     https://www.specialeducationnotes.in

🔲 **Aphasia** – Loss of ability to understand or express speech due to brain damage.
🎤 **Voice Disorders** – Hoarseness, loss of voice, or abnormal pitch due to vocal cord problems.

🔴 How Does This Disability Affect Life?

✅ **Difficulty in Expressing Thoughts** – Struggles in verbal communication.
✅ **Challenges in Social Interaction** – Fear of speaking leads to isolation.
✅ **Educational Barriers** – Difficulty in reading, writing, and participating in class.
✅ **Limited Job Opportunities** – Many professions require effective communication.
✅ **Emotional Impact** – Anxiety, frustration, and loss of confidence.

💡 **Example:** A child with **stammering** may hesitate to speak in class, affecting their confidence and learning progress.

🛠 Treatment & Management

🔷 **Speech Therapy** – Helps improve pronunciation and fluency.
🔷 **Assistive Communication Devices** – Picture boards, text-to-speech apps.
🔷 **Sign Language & Alternative Communication Methods** – Used for severe cases.
🔷 **Psychological Support** – Helps in overcoming social anxiety.
🔷 **Special Education Programs** – Tailored learning methods for speech-impaired students.

🎯 Government Support & Benefits

📚 **Special Learning Support** – Modified teaching methods and exam accommodations.
💼 **Job Reservations** – Opportunities in government jobs for persons with disabilities.
🏥 **Medical & Therapy Support** – Free/subsidized treatment in disability centers.
💰 **Financial Aid & Disability Pension** – Support for those with severe impairments.

🌟 Inspiring Story – Triumph Over Speech Challenges!

✨ **Joe Biden**, the President of the United States, struggled with **stammering** in his childhood but overcame it through practice and determination, proving that a speech disability doesn't define success!

🚀 Final Thought:

Speech and Language Disabilities can **make communication difficult, but with therapy, technology, and proper support, individuals can thrive** in their personal and professional lives.

1 7 Thalassemia – A Battle in the Blood

📌 What is Thalassemia?

Thalassemia is a **genetic blood disorder** where the body **produces less hemoglobin than normal**, leading to **severe anemia, fatigue, and organ damage**. It requires **lifelong medical care**, including blood transfusions and medications.

📜 Definition as per RPWD Act, 2016

A **chronic blood disorder** that results in **low hemoglobin levels**, affecting oxygen transport in the body, causing **fatigue, weakness, and other complications**.

🔔 Why Does It Happen?

🧬 **Genetic Disorder** – Passed from parents to children due to abnormal genes.
🩸 **Defective Hemoglobin Production** – Red blood cells cannot carry enough oxygen.
⚫ **Most Common in Certain Regions** – High cases in **Mediterranean, Middle East, South Asia**.
👁 **Can Be Detected Before Birth** – Through prenatal genetic tests.
⏳ **Lifelong Condition** – No permanent cure except **bone marrow transplant** in some cases.

🔍 Types of Thalassemia

1 **Thalassemia Minor** – Mild form, may not need treatment.
2 **Thalassemia Intermedia** – Moderate anemia, may require occasional treatment.
3 **Thalassemia Major (Cooley's Anemia)** – Severe form, requires **regular blood transfusions** for survival.

🩸 How Does It Affect Life?

☑ **Extreme Fatigue & Weakness** – Due to insufficient oxygen in the blood.
☑ **Delayed Growth & Development** – Especially in children.

☑ **Frequent Blood Transfusions Needed** – Can lead to **iron overload** in the body.
☑ **Bone Deformities & Organ Damage** – Due to excess iron deposits.
☑ **Increased Risk of Infections** – Weak immune system due to frequent hospital visits.

💡 **Example:** A child with **Thalassemia Major** may require **monthly blood transfusions** and iron chelation therapy to survive.

✂ Treatment & Management

◆ **Regular Blood Transfusions** – To maintain healthy hemoglobin levels.
◆ **Iron Chelation Therapy** – Removes excess iron from the body.
◆ **Bone Marrow Transplant** – The only possible permanent cure (in selected cases).
◆ **Healthy Diet & Lifestyle** – To prevent complications.
◆ **Gene Therapy (Experimental)** – Future hope for a cure.

🎯 Government Support & Benefits

🏥 **Free or Subsidized Blood Transfusions** in government hospitals.
📚 **Education & Job Reservations** for persons with disabilities.
🩺 **Financial Aid & Health Insurance** for treatment costs.
🏛 **Research & Awareness Programs** to support better treatment options.

🔥 Real-Life Inspiration – A Fighter's Story!

✴ **Zaynab Moghal**, a young Thalassemia warrior, has been spreading awareness about the condition and proving that **with the right support, patients can lead fulfilling lives.**

🚀 Final Thought:

Thalassemia **is challenging, but with proper treatment, care, and government support, individuals can live a long and active life.**

🔢 Hemophilia – The Disorder of Unstoppable Bleeding

📌 What is Hemophilia?

Hemophilia is a **genetic bleeding disorder** where the **blood does not clot properly**, leading to **excessive bleeding from even minor injuries**. In severe cases, **internal bleeding in joints and organs** can be life-threatening.

📜 Definition as per RPWD Act, 2016

A **hereditary disorder** where the blood **lacks clotting factors**, resulting in **prolonged bleeding and severe complications**.

🔔 What Causes Hemophilia?

🧬 **Genetic Mutation** – Passed from parents due to defective genes.
💧 **Lack of Clotting Factors** – Blood lacks **Factor VIII (Hemophilia A)** or **Factor IX (Hemophilia B)**.
🧑‍⚕️ **Rarely Acquired** – Can develop later due to **immune system disorders**.
👦 **Affects Mostly Males** – Women are usually carriers but rarely affected.
🔄 **No Permanent Cure** – But it can be **managed with lifelong treatment**.

🔍 Types of Hemophilia

1. **Hemophilia A** – Caused by a deficiency of **Factor VIII**, most common type.
2. **Hemophilia B (Christmas Disease)** – Caused by **Factor IX deficiency**.
3. **Hemophilia C** – Rare, due to **Factor XI deficiency**, affects both genders.

💧 How Does It Affect Life?

✅ **Excessive Bleeding** – Even a small cut can take a long time to stop bleeding.
✅ **Internal Bleeding in Joints** – Causes **swelling, pain, and joint damage**.
✅ **Risk of Brain Hemorrhage** – A head injury can be **fatal**.
✅ **Frequent Need for Clotting Factor Injections** – Regular medical care is required.
✅ **Limitations in Physical Activities** – Contact sports can be dangerous.

💡 **Example:** A child with **Hemophilia A** might get **severe bruises from minor falls** and need **immediate clotting factor injections**.

✂ Treatment & Management

◆ **Clotting Factor Replacement Therapy** – Infusions of missing clotting factors.
◆ **Desmopressin (DDAVP)** – A medicine to boost clotting factor levels in mild cases.
◆ **Avoiding Injury-Prone Activities** – Reducing the risk of excessive bleeding.
◆ **Regular Physiotherapy** – To prevent joint damage from internal bleeding.
◆ **Gene Therapy (Future Treatment)** – Research is ongoing for a **permanent cure**.

◎ Government Support & Benefits

▥ **Free or Subsidized Factor Replacement Therapy** in public hospitals.
▤ **Education & Job Reservations** to ensure financial independence.
▨ **Disability Pension & Financial Aid** for lifelong treatment.
▥ **Awareness Programs** to improve early diagnosis and care.

◍ Real-Life Inspiration – A Hemophilia Warrior!

✿ **Ryan White**, an American activist with Hemophilia, fought for **healthcare rights** and inspired millions despite his challenges.

◿ Final Thought:

Though **Hemophilia is a lifelong condition, proper treatment and lifestyle adjustments** allow individuals to **lead normal and active lives**.

1 9 ◊ Sickle Cell Disease – The Shape That Changes Everything!

🔍 What is Sickle Cell Disease (SCD)?

Sickle Cell Disease is a **genetic blood disorder** where **red blood cells become crescent (sickle)-shaped instead of round**. These abnormally shaped cells **clump together, block blood flow, and cause severe pain, organ damage, and anemia.**

▱ Think of it like this:
● **Normal red blood cells** = Smooth, flexible, travel easily through blood vessels.
● **Sickle-shaped cells** = Stiff, sticky, cause blockages, leading to pain and organ damage.

📜 RPWD Act, 2016 Definition

A **hereditary blood disorder** where **abnormal hemoglobin** causes **misshapen red blood cells**, leading to **pain crises, organ damage, and reduced oxygen supply** to tissues.

⚠ Why Does SCD Happen?

🧬 **Genetic Mutation** – Passed from parents through defective genes.
💧 **Abnormal Hemoglobin (HbS)** – Makes red blood cells rigid and sickle-shaped.
⚫ **Most Common in Certain Ethnic Groups** – High cases in **Africa, India, Middle East**.
⏳ **Lifelong Condition** – Can only be cured with a **bone marrow transplant** (rare).
🔲 **Sickle Cell Trait vs. Disease** – If you inherit one sickle gene, you're a carrier; if you inherit two, you have the disease.

💥 How Does SCD Affect Life?

☑ **Sudden Pain Attacks ("Sickle Cell Crisis")** – Severe pain in **bones, chest, and abdomen**.
☑ **Frequent Infections** – Weak immune system, increased risk of pneumonia & stroke.
☑ **Chronic Fatigue & Anemia** – Due to **shortened lifespan of sickle cells**.
☑ **Delayed Growth & Puberty** – Affects development in children.
☑ **Organ Damage Over Time** – Heart, kidney, liver, and brain complications.

💡 **Example:** A person with SCD may suddenly experience **excruciating pain in their limbs**, needing **hospitalization for oxygen and pain management**.

🔧 How is it Managed?

◆ **Pain Management** – Strong painkillers (opioids) for sickle cell crises.
◆ **Blood Transfusions** – Help increase normal red blood cell count.
◆ **Hydroxyurea Medication** – Reduces pain attacks and improves blood flow.
◆ **Stem Cell Transplant** – **Potential cure**, but only for selected cases.
◆ **Preventive Care** – Avoid **cold weather, dehydration, and infections** to prevent crises.

⊚ Government Support & Benefits

🔋 **Free Medical Treatment** – Blood transfusions & medications in government hospitals.
📚 **Education & Job Reservations** – Support for affected individuals.
💰 **Financial Aid & Disability Pension** – Monthly assistance for severe cases.
⚗️ **Research & Awareness Programs** – To improve early diagnosis and treatment.

🔥 A True Fighter's Story!

✨ **Tionne "T-Boz" Watkins**, a member of the famous music group **TLC**, has battled Sickle Cell Disease since childhood but still became a successful singer and activist! 🎤✨

🚀 Final Thought:

Sickle Cell Disease **is painful and lifelong**, but with **proper medical care, lifestyle changes, and support**, people with SCD **can live full and productive lives**.

2 0 🔥 Multiple Disabilities – When Challenges Multiply!

🔍 What Are Multiple Disabilities?

Multiple Disabilities refer to a **combination of two or more disabilities** in a single individual, making daily life and rehabilitation **more complex**.

📖 Imagine this:
A person who is both **blind and has cerebral palsy**.
A child who has **autism and hearing impairment**.
Managing just one disability is tough—now imagine dealing with two or more at the same time!

📜 RPWD Act, 2016 Definition

A person with **two or more disabilities from the list of 21 disabilities** under the RPWD Act. These combined impairments **create unique challenges in mobility, learning, communication, and daily activities**.

⚠️ Why Do Multiple Disabilities Occur?

🦴 **Genetic Disorders** – Conditions like **Down Syndrome** can cause multiple disabilities.
🧴 **Birth Complications** – Lack of oxygen at birth can lead to **cerebral palsy + visual impairment**.
💊 **Infections & Diseases** – Meningitis can result in **hearing loss + intellectual disability**.
🙁 **Accidents & Injuries** – A traumatic brain injury might cause **physical + cognitive disabilities**.

💥 How Do Multiple Disabilities Affect Life?

☑️ **Limited Communication Ability** – A child who is both **deaf and intellectually disabled** may struggle to express needs.
☑️ **Mobility Challenges** – Someone with **blindness and cerebral palsy** may require a wheelchair and a guide.
☑️ **Learning Barriers** – Traditional education may not work; special techniques are needed.
☑️ **Dependence on Caregivers** – Many individuals need **24/7 support** for daily tasks.
☑️ **Delayed Social Development** – Difficulty in interacting with others due to combined impairments.

💡 **Example:** A student who has **autism and is non-verbal** will need **special education techniques, assistive technology, and therapy** to communicate and learn effectively.

🛠️ How is it Managed?

◆ **Individualized Education Plan (IEP)** – Special teaching methods tailored to needs.
◆ **Assistive Technologies** – Braille devices, speech-to-text apps, mobility aids.
◆ **Physical & Speech Therapy** – To improve movement and communication.
◆ **Multi-Sensory Learning** – Combining **touch, sound, visuals, and movement** to aid learning.
◆ **Specialized Care Centers** – Schools & rehab centers designed for multiple disabilities.

🎯 Government Support & Benefits

🏥 **Special Health & Rehab Programs** – Free therapy & assistive devices.
📚 **Inclusive Education Policies** – Schools must accommodate multiple disabilities.
💰 **Disability Pension & Job Reservations** – Financial aid for affected individuals.
👩 **Legal Guardianship & Caregiver Support** – For those needing lifelong care.

🔥 A Real-Life Inspiration!

✳️ **Helen Keller** – Deafblind from childhood, she became an **author, educator, and activist**, proving that multiple disabilities do not limit success!

🚀 Final Thought:

People with multiple disabilities face **unique challenges**, but with **specialized support, education, and assistive technology**, they can lead meaningful and independent lives.

2 1 🔥 Acid Attack Victims – Strength Beyond Scars!

🔍 Who Are Acid Attack Victims?

Acid attack victims are individuals who have suffered **severe burns, disfigurement, and disabilities** due to the intentional use of **corrosive substances** like acid. These attacks not only **cause physical pain** but also lead to **psychological trauma and social discrimination**.

🖼️ Imagine This:
A young woman, once full of dreams, becomes a victim of an acid attack.
She survives, but her **face is disfigured, vision is affected, and mobility is limited** due to burns.
Despite this, she fights back, rebuilds her life, and inspires thousands!

📜 RPWD Act, 2016 Definition

A person suffering from **disfigurement or disability** caused by an acid attack, which may affect their **mobility, vision, speech, or psychological health**.

⚠️ What Are the Consequences of an Acid Attack?

🩹 **Severe Skin Burns** – Can lead to **permanent scarring and disfigurement**.
👁️ **Vision Loss** – Many victims experience **partial or complete blindness**.
🧠 **Mental Trauma & PTSD** – Emotional distress, depression, and anxiety.
🦴 **Restricted Mobility** – Burnt skin tightens over time, making movement difficult.
👥 **Social Stigma & Discrimination** – Victims often face **job loss, rejection, and isolation**.

💡 **Example:** A girl attacked with acid at 18 lost her vision and struggled with depression but later became a **motivational speaker and social activist**!

🔧 How Can It Be Managed?

◆ **Multiple Surgeries & Skin Grafts** – To restore **functionality and appearance**.
◆ **Counseling & Psychological Support** – To heal from **trauma and social rejection**.
◆ **Specialized Eye Treatments** – For those who lose vision due to acid damage.
◆ **Rehabilitation & Skill Training** – Helps victims **gain financial independence**.
◆ **Legal & Police Support** – **Strict laws** to punish attackers and protect victims.

🎯 Government Support & Benefits

Free Medical Treatment & Plastic Surgeries in government hospitals.
Compensation Scheme – Up to **₹3 lakh** for survivors.
Job Reservations & Educational Support for acid attack victims.
Housing & Financial Assistance for rehabilitation.
Strict Laws – India has toughened laws with **10 years to life imprisonment** for attackers.

🔥 A True Fighter's Story!

Laxmi Agarwal, an acid attack survivor, became an **activist, TV host, and TED speaker**. Her story inspired the Bollywood film **"Chhapaak"**, proving that **courage is stronger than cruelty!**

🚀 Final Thought:

Acid attack victims are **not just survivors—they are warriors!** With **proper support, rehabilitation, and societal acceptance**, they can **live with dignity and achieve their dreams**.

📌 Practice Questions on RPWD Act, 2016

1.On which date the RPwD Act, 2016 was implemented in India?

Ⓐ 1 January 2016
Ⓑ 15 August 2016
Ⓒ 19 April 2017
Ⓓ 3 December 2016

✅ **Answer:** Ⓒ 19 April 2017

💡 **Trick to Remember:**

- **RPwD Act, 2016 was enacted on 28 December 2016** 📜

- **It came into effect on 19 April 2017** 🔥

2.How many types of disabilities are included in the RPwD Act, 2016?

Ⓐ 7
Ⓑ 14
Ⓒ 21
Ⓓ 27

✅ **Answer:** Ⓒ 21

💡 **Memory Tip: Earlier there were 7, now there are 21! That means 7 x 3 = 21, you can remember it from here.**

3.What is the definition of 'Blindness' as per RPwD Act?

Ⓐ When the visual capacity is 6/60 or less
Ⓑ When the person cannot distinguish between colours
Ⓒ When the visual field is 10 degrees or less
Ⓓ Only congenital blindness

✅ **Answer: ●When the visual field is 10 degrees or less**

💡 **Extra Fact: Blindness also includes Visual Acuity <3/60!**

---

4. Which of the following is a 'mental' disability recognized by the RPwD Act, 2016?

Ⓐ Heart Disease
Ⓑ Epilepsy
Ⓒ Asthma
Ⓓ Hypertension

✅ **Answer: ● Epilepsy**

💡 **Mnemonic Trick:** 💭 **"CIM" i.e. Cerebral Palsy, Intellectual Disability, Mental Illness, all three are related to mental disabilities!**

5. What percentage of reservation is given to handicapped people in government jobs?

Ⓐ 2%
Ⓑ 3%
Ⓒ 4%
Ⓓ 5%

✅ **Answer: Ⓓ 5%**

💡 **Remember:Earlier it was 3%, now it has been made 5%!** 🚀

6. What does "Inclusive Education" mean?

Ⓐ Teaching disabled children in a separate school from normal children   Ⓑ Teaching
disabled and normal children together   Ⓒ Teaching
disabled children only in special schools
Ⓓ Providing special facilities only to blind children

✅ **Answer: Ⓑ Teaching disabled and normal children together**

💡 **Extra Knowledge: The National Policy on Education (NPE) in India also emphasizes on inclusive education.**

7. Who is responsible for implementing the 'Equal Opportunity Policy' under the RPwD Act, 2016?

Ⓐ Central Government
Ⓑ State Government
Ⓒ Private Companies and Government Offices   Ⓓ
Voluntary Organizations of Persons with Disabilities Only

✅ **Answer: Ⓒ Private Companies and Government Offices**

💡 **Trick: Wherever it comes to "Equal Opportunity", the company and government departments are responsible!**

8. Who issues a Disability Certificate?

Ⓐ Any doctor
Ⓑ Panchayat Samiti
Ⓒ Medical board of any hospital
Ⓓ Government Medical Board

✅ **Answer: Ⓓ Government Medical Board**

💡 **Tip: Only Govt. Medical Board can issue the certificate!**

---

9. What is the main objective of 'Accessible India Campaign'?

Ⓐ Making government schemes for disabled persons
Ⓑ Creating a barrier-free environment for disabled persons
Ⓒ Giving special reservation to disabled persons
Ⓓ Providing free health facilities to disabled persons

✅ **Answer: Ⓑ Creating a barrier-free environment for differently abled people**

💡 **Trick: "Accessible" means increasing accessibility!**

---

10. When did 'Sign Language' get official recognition?

Ⓐ 2010
Ⓑ 2015
Ⓒ 2020
Ⓓ 2021

✅ **Answer: Ⓓ 2021**

💡 **Extra Fact: India recognized Indian Sign Language (ISL) in 2021!**

Introduction

ADHD (Attention Deficit Hyperactivity Disorder) and Autism Spectrum Disorder (ASD) are two neurodevelopmental disorders that significantly impact a child's ability to learn and interact with their surroundings. While ADHD is characterized by inattention, hyperactivity, and impulsivity, Autism is marked by challenges in social interaction, communication, and repetitive behaviors.

Attention Deficit Hyperactivity Disorder (ADHD)

Definition:

ADHD is a chronic condition that affects millions of children and often continues into adulthood. It includes persistent patterns of inattention, hyperactivity, and impulsivity that interfere with functioning or development.

Causes:

- **Genetic Factors:** Family history of ADHD
- **Neurological Factors:** Differences in brain structure and function
- **Environmental Factors:** Lead exposure, prenatal drug/alcohol use
- **Dietary Factors:** Artificial food coloring, sugar (not scientifically proven but assumed)

Characteristics:

Domain	Symptoms
Inattention	Easily distracted, forgetful, poor focus, avoids tasks requiring attention
Hyperactivity	Fidgeting, excessive talking, difficulty staying seated, restlessness
Impulsivity	Interrupts others, difficulty waiting for a turn, acts without thinking

Educational Strategies:

- **Classroom Modifications:** Flexible seating, structured routine
- **Behavioral Interventions:** Token economy, reward system
- **Instructional Strategies:** Multi-sensory teaching, breaking tasks into small steps
- **Use of Technology:** Apps for focus improvement, visual timers

- 🐻 **Collaboration:** Teachers, parents, and therapists working together

---

Autism Spectrum Disorder (ASD)

Definition:

Autism Spectrum Disorder (ASD) is a developmental disorder that affects communication and behavior. It is called a "spectrum" because symptoms vary widely among individuals.

Causes: 🧩

- **Genetic Factors:** Mutations in certain genes
- **Neurological Factors:** Brain connectivity issues 🧠
- **Environmental Factors:** Prenatal infections, parental age 🧬

Characteristics: ✴

Domain	Symptoms
Social Interaction	Avoids eye contact, struggles with social cues, prefers isolation
Communication	Delayed speech, repetitive language, difficulty understanding sarcasm
Behavior	Repetitive actions (hand-flapping, rocking), strict adherence to routines

Educational Strategies: 🎓

- 📋 **Structured Learning Environment:** Visual schedules, predictable routines
- 🖐 **Communication Support:** PECS (Picture Exchange Communication System), Augmentative & Alternative Communication (AAC)
- 😊 **Social Skills Training:** Role-playing, peer modeling
- 🧸 **Sensory Integration:** Calming corners, weighted blankets
- 🏛 **Specialized Teaching Methods:** Applied Behavior Analysis (ABA), TEACCH approach

---

Comparison: ADHD vs. Autism

Feature	ADHD	Autism
Attention Issues	Yes	Sometimes
Hyperactivity	Yes	Rarely
Social Skills	Impaired but interested in socializing	Difficulty in social interaction
Communication Delay	No	Yes
Repetitive Behaviors	No	Yes
Response to Change	Adapts quickly	Resists change

Government Policies & Initiatives in India 🏛️

- 🧾 **The Rights of Persons with Disabilities Act, 2016** – Recognizes ASD and ADHD as disabilities.
- 🏛️ **Sarva Shiksha Abhiyan (SSA)** – Ensures inclusive education.
- 📘 **National Policy for Persons with Disabilities, 2006** – Promotes special education.
- 🧴 **Inclusive Education for Disabled at Secondary Stage (IEDSS)** – Provides financial support.

Exam-Oriented MCQs & PYQs 🎯

1 Which of the following is NOT a symptom of ADHD?
a) Inattention
b) Hyperactivity
c) Repetitive behaviors
d) Impulsivity
✅ **Answer: c) Repetitive behaviors**

2 The Picture Exchange Communication System (PECS) is used for children with:
a) ADHD
b) Autism
c) Dyslexia
d) Down Syndrome
✅ **Answer: b) Autism**

3 **Which of the following is a recommended teaching strategy for children with ADHD?**
a) Long lectures
b) Multi-sensory approach
c) Ignoring hyperactivity
d) Restrictive classroom setup
Answer: b) Multi-sensory approach

Education of Mentally Retarded, Physically Handicapped & Hearing/Vision Impaired Children

Introduction

Inclusive education ensures that children with disabilities receive appropriate support to learn and grow alongside their peers. This section covers the education of children with **Intellectual Disabilities (Mentally Retarded), Physically Handicapped, and Hearing/Vision Impaired** students, highlighting their unique needs and teaching strategies.

Education of Mentally Retarded (Intellectually Disabled) Children

Definition:

Intellectual Disability (formerly Mental Retardation) is a neurodevelopmental disorder characterized by **below-average intellectual functioning (IQ < 70) and deficits in adaptive behaviors** (social, practical, and conceptual skills).

Causes:

- **Genetic Factors:** Down Syndrome, Fragile X Syndrome
- **Prenatal Causes:** Fetal alcohol syndrome, infections during pregnancy
- **Perinatal Causes:** Birth asphyxia, low birth weight
- **Postnatal Causes:** Brain infections, head trauma

Characteristics:

Domain	Challenges Faced
Cognitive	Slow learning, difficulty in problem-solving
Social	Difficulty understanding social norms, poor communication
Motor Skills	Delayed development, clumsiness
Academic	Struggles with reading, writing, math

Educational Strategies:

- **Repetition-Based Learning:** Frequent reinforcement
- **Multi-Sensory Teaching:** Visual, auditory, and kinesthetic learning
- **Task Analysis:** Breaking tasks into smaller steps
- **Life Skills Training:** Focus on self-care and vocational skills
- **Peer Support:** Collaborative learning with non-disabled peers

---

Education of Physically Handicapped Children

Definition:

Physically Handicapped (Orthopedic Impairment) children have **mobility limitations** due to conditions like **cerebral palsy, muscular dystrophy, polio, and spinal cord injuries.**

Causes:

- **Congenital Factors:** Spina bifida, clubfoot
- **Neuromuscular Disorders:** Cerebral palsy, muscular dystrophy
- **Injury-Related:** Accidents, spinal cord damage

Challenges in Education:

Domain	Challenges Faced
Mobility	Difficulty accessing classrooms, writing, physical activity
Social	Feelings of isolation, lack of participation
Communication	Some may have speech impairments

Educational Strategies: 🎓

- 🏛️ **Barrier-Free Infrastructure:** Ramps, elevators, accessible desks
- 📝 **Assistive Devices:** Adaptive keyboards, voice-to-text software
- 🧩 **Individualized Education Plan (IEP):** Customized learning goals
- 💪 **Physical Therapy & Adaptive PE:** Strength training, modified sports
- 💡 **Alternative Communication Methods:** If speech is affected, use AAC devices

---

Education of Hearing & Vision Impaired Children

Hearing Impairment 🎧

Definition:

Hearing Impairment refers to **partial or complete hearing loss** affecting communication and learning. It can be **mild, moderate, severe, or profound.**

Causes: 🎵

- **Genetic:** Hereditary deafness
- **Infections:** Maternal rubella, meningitis
- **Environmental:** Noise exposure, ototoxic drugs

Challenges in Education:

Domain	Challenges Faced
Communication	Difficulty understanding spoken language
Social	Limited peer interaction
Learning	Struggles with oral instruction

Educational Strategies: 📖

- 🤚 **Sign Language & Speech Therapy:** Indian Sign Language (ISL), lip-reading
- 📺 **Visual Aids & Captioning:** Subtitled videos, real-time transcription
- 🎙 **FM Systems & Hearing Aids:** Enhancing sound perception
- 📋 **Special Schools & Resource Teachers:** Focus on auditory-verbal training

---

Vision Impairment 👓

Definition:

Vision Impairment refers to **partial or complete loss of sight** that cannot be corrected fully by glasses.

Causes: 👁

- **Congenital:** Retinopathy of prematurity, albinism
- **Acquired:** Glaucoma, cataracts, optic nerve damage

Challenges in Education:

Domain	Challenges Faced
Reading	Difficulty in reading normal-sized text
Mobility	Trouble navigating in unfamiliar spaces
Classroom Learning	Difficulty accessing written material

Educational Strategies: 🏫

- 📚 **Braille & Large Print Books:** Alternative reading formats
- 🔊 **Audio Books & Screen Readers:** JAWS, NVDA software
- ✏ **Orientation & Mobility Training:** Cane use, echolocation techniques
- 🎯 **High-Contrast & Tactile Materials:** Raised diagrams, bold fonts

---

Government Policies & Initiatives in India 🏛

- 📜 **The Rights of Persons with Disabilities Act, 2016** – Mandates inclusive education.
- 🏫 **Sarva Shiksha Abhiyan (SSA)** – Special educators & learning aids.
- 📘 **National Policy for Persons with Disabilities, 2006** – Promotes accessibility.
- 💰 **Scholarships & Financial Aid:** Incentives for special education.

Exam-Oriented MCQs & PYQs 🎯

1 What is the primary characteristic of Intellectual Disability?
a) Difficulty in motor coordination
b) Below-average intellectual functioning
c) Hyperactivity
d) Advanced cognitive skills
✅ **Answer: b) Below-average intellectual functioning**

2 Which assistive device is most useful for visually impaired students?
a) FM system
b) Braille books
c) Speech-to-text software
d) Hearing aids
✅ **Answer: b) Braille books**

3 What does an FM system help with?
a) Improving motor skills
b) Enhancing sound clarity for hearing-impaired students
c) Teaching Braille to visually impaired students
d) Assisting physically disabled students in movement
✅ **Answer: b) Enhancing sound clarity for hearing-impaired students**

📑 *Education of Socially & Economically Disadvantaged Children* ⚪

🚀 Breaking Barriers: The Struggle & Solutions for Disadvantaged Children

Children from socially and economically disadvantaged backgrounds often face **deep-rooted challenges** in accessing quality education. **Limited resources, cultural constraints, and financial instability** create obstacles that hinder their academic growth. This section delves into their struggles and explores **effective strategies** to ensure education for all. 🎓✨

⚠ Challenges Faced by Socially & Economically Disadvantaged Children

🏗 Challenge	📉 Impact on Education
👛 Poverty & Financial Hardships	Leads to school dropouts, child labor, and poor academic performance.
🚹 Gender & Social Discrimination	Girls and children from marginalized communities face fewer educational opportunities.
🏚 Poor Infrastructure & Resources	Lack of basic amenities like classrooms, books, and digital tools.
🗣 Language & Cultural Barriers	Non-native language instruction leads to comprehension issues.
🏠 Lack of Parental Awareness	Parents with low literacy levels may not prioritize formal education.

🎯 Strategies to Improve Education for Disadvantaged Children

1 Financial & Social Empowerment 👛

- 🏫 **Free & Subsidized Education:** Ensuring education is not a financial burden.
- 🍽 **Mid-Day Meal Scheme:** Providing meals to improve attendance and concentration.
- ✂ **Vocational Training Programs:** Equipping students with job-ready skills.

2 Inclusive & Engaging Learning Methods 📖

- 🗣 **Bilingual Education:** Teaching in regional languages for better understanding.
- 🧠 **Activity-Based Learning:** Encouraging interactive and skill-based teaching.
- 📚 **Specialized Remedial Programs:** Additional classes for students needing extra support.

3 Strengthening Infrastructure & Digital Access 🏫

- 🏫 **Upgrading Schools:** Building better classrooms, libraries, and computer labs.
- 💻 **Technology-Enabled Learning:** Providing tablets, e-books, and virtual classrooms.
- 🚌 **Mobile & Community Schools:** Taking education to remote and underprivileged areas.

4 Government & Community Intervention 🏛️

- 📖 **Community Involvement:** Encouraging local groups to support schooling.
- 🎓 **Scholarships & Incentives:** Ensuring financial aid reaches deserving students.
- 🛡️ **Public-Private Partnerships:** Collaborating with NGOs and private organizations to enhance school quality.

📜 Government Policies & Initiatives in India

🏛️ Policy/Initiative	🎯 Objective
🟦 Right to Education (RTE) Act, 2009	Ensures free & compulsory education for children aged 6-14.
🍽️ Mid-Day Meal Scheme	Improves school attendance and nutritional status.
🏫 Samagra Shiksha Abhiyan (SSA)	Strengthens school infrastructure and teacher training.
💰 National Means-Cum-Merit Scholarship (NMMS)	Provides financial aid to meritorious students from economically weak backgrounds.
👧 Beti Bachao, Beti Padhao	Promotes girls' education and empowerment.

🎯 Exam-Oriented MCQs & PYQs

1 Which of the following is a key reason for school dropouts among underprivileged children?
a) Overcrowded classrooms
b) Lack of financial support
c) Strict school discipline
d) Availability of better jobs
✅ **Answer: b) Lack of financial support**

2 What is the primary goal of the Right to Education Act?
a) Providing higher education scholarships
b) Ensuring free and compulsory education for children
c) Supporting only rural students
d) Privatizing government schools
✅ **Answer: b) Ensuring free and compulsory education for children**

3 **How does the Mid-Day Meal Scheme benefit students?**
a) Encourages school attendance by providing meals
b) Reduces teacher workload
c) Increases syllabus coverage
d) Provides employment to local farmers
✓ **Answer: a) Encourages school attendance by providing meals**

4 **What role does bilingual education play in helping disadvantaged children?**
a) Encourages rote learning
b) Helps children understand subjects in their native language
c) Reduces the importance of English
d) Limits access to higher education
✓ **Answer: b) Helps children understand subjects in their native language**

5 **Why are public-private partnerships important in the education sector?**
a) They make education more expensive
b) They help improve school quality and resources
c) They replace government schools
d) They focus only on urban education
✓ **Answer: b) They help improve school quality and resources**

3 Policies, Acts & Laws Related to Special Education

📚 *Rights of Persons with Disabilities (RPWD) Act, 2016*

🔍 **Understanding the RPWD Act, 2016**

The **Rights of Persons with Disabilities (RPWD) Act, 2016** was enacted to uphold the **rights, dignity, and inclusion** of persons with disabilities (PwDs) in India. It replaces the **Persons with Disabilities (Equal Opportunities, Protection of Rights and Full Participation) Act, 1995** and aligns with the **United Nations Convention on the Rights of Persons with Disabilities (UNCRPD).** 🌐✨

The primary objective of this Act is to **empower individuals with disabilities** by ensuring equal opportunities in education, employment, social security, and accessibility to public spaces. It mandates **strict legal provisions** against discrimination and promotes **inclusive development** of PwDs in all spheres of life.

📜 Key Provisions of the RPWD Act, 2016

📌 Provision	🔍 Description
Increased Disability Categories	Expands recognized disabilities from **7 to 21**, including autism, learning disabilities, and mental illnesses.
Education Rights 🎓	Mandates **free education** for children with benchmark disabilities (≥40% disability) between ages 6-18 in neighborhood schools and special schools.
Reservation in Higher Education & Jobs 🏫💼	Increases reservation for PwDs from **3% to 4%** in government jobs and **5%** in higher education institutions, ensuring better representation and inclusion.
Accessible Infrastructure 🏢	Ensures public spaces, transport, and workplaces are **barrier-free** and **disabled-friendly**, including ramps, Braille signage, and assistive technologies.
Employment Protection 🧑	Prohibits discrimination in employment and mandates workplace accommodations such as **flexible work hours, assistive technologies, and barrier-free access** for PwDs.
Legal Rights & Guardianship ⚖️	Provides **legal recognition** of guardianship, ensuring PwDs have decision-making support through either an **appointed guardian or assisted decision-making models**.
Social Security & Welfare 🏅	Introduces **pension schemes, insurance benefits, and financial aid** for PwDs to ensure economic stability and well-being.
Penalties for Violations 🔔	Imposes **fines, imprisonment, and penalties** for individuals, institutions, or organizations found violating the rights of PwDs.

🎯 Key Features & Impact of the RPWD Act

1️⃣ Expansion of Disability Categories 🧩

- The Act significantly broadens the **scope of disabilities** by increasing the number of recognized disabilities from **7 to 21**. This now includes:
    - **Neurological disorders** (e.g., Autism Spectrum Disorder, Parkinson's Disease)
    - **Blood disorders** (e.g., Hemophilia, Thalassemia, Sickle Cell Disease)
    - **Learning disabilities** (e.g., Dyslexia, Dyscalculia, Dysgraphia)
    - **Psychiatric disabilities** (e.g., Depression, Schizophrenia)

2 Strengthening Educational Rights 📖

- **Right to Inclusive Education:** All educational institutions must ensure equal learning opportunities and **provide assistive technologies, special educators, and modified curriculums** to accommodate students with disabilities.
- **Scholarships & Support Programs:** Financial assistance is provided for PwDs to continue higher education.
- **Special Provisions for Examinations:** Additional time, scribes, and alternative exam formats must be made available for students with disabilities.

3 Employment & Economic Empowerment 💼

- **4% Reservation in Government Jobs:** This includes **public sector organizations and local bodies** to increase the workforce participation of PwDs.
- **Skill Development Programs:** Vocational training, self-employment support, and entrepreneurial assistance programs are encouraged under the Act.
- **No Discrimination in the Workplace:** Employers must ensure **reasonable accommodations**, accessible workplaces, and non-discriminatory hiring practices.

4 Accessibility & Barrier-Free Environment 🖼️ 👤

- **Public spaces, transport systems, and digital platforms** must be designed to ensure accessibility.
- **Mandatory accessibility audits** for government and private buildings to ensure compliance with universal design principles.
- **Access to Assistive Technologies:** Providing wheelchairs, hearing aids, Braille materials, and digital assistive tools for daily use.

5 Legal Rights & Protection Against Discrimination ⚖️

- **Stronger Legal Remedies:** Victims of discrimination or harassment based on disability can seek legal action.
- **Special Courts for PwDs:** Establishment of courts to deal with cases of rights violations efficiently.
- **Right to Guardianship:** Individuals with severe disabilities can have **nominated guardians** or **self-appointed legal support persons** to assist in decision-making.

📚 Exam-Oriented MCQs & PYQs

1 The RPWD Act, 2016 increased the number of recognized disabilities from:
a) 7 to 14
b) 7 to 21

c) 10 to 25
d) 15 to 30
☑ **Answer: b) 7 to 21**

2 **Which of the following rights is provided under the RPWD Act, 2016?**
a) Free education for all PwDs in private schools
b) Reservation in government jobs and higher education
c) Exclusive employment rights in private sector companies
d) Mandatory home schooling for all PwDs
☑ **Answer: b) Reservation in government jobs and higher education**

3 **What percentage of reservation is provided for PwDs in higher education institutions?**
a) 2%
b) 3%
c) 5%
d) 6%
☑ **Answer: c) 5%**

4 **What does the RPWD Act mandate regarding accessibility?**
a) Only schools must be accessible
b) Public spaces, transport, and ICT must be accessible
c) Only government offices must be accessible
d) Accessibility is optional
☑ **Answer: b) Public spaces, transport, and ICT must be accessible**

5 **What is the consequence of violating the RPWD Act?**
a) No action is taken
b) Monetary fines and possible imprisonment
c) Only a warning is issued
d) The violator has to apologize publicly
☑ **Answer: b) Monetary fines and possible imprisonment**

📚 National Education Policy (NEP) 2020 & Inclusive Education

🎇 Overview of NEP 2020 & Its Approach to Inclusive Education

The **National Education Policy (NEP) 2020** is a transformative policy aimed at overhauling the Indian education system to make it **more holistic, flexible, multidisciplinary, and inclusive**. The policy emphasizes **equity and accessibility** for all learners, especially those from disadvantaged backgrounds, including **Children with Disabilities (CWDs)**. 🎓 🎇

NEP 2020 aims to ensure that students with disabilities are **fully integrated into mainstream education**, promoting **Universal Design for Learning (UDL), assistive technologies, and specialized support systems** to enhance accessibility.

📑 Key Provisions of NEP 2020 for Inclusive Education

📌 Provision	🔍 Description
Early Childhood Care & Education (ECCE)	Focuses on **early intervention** for children with disabilities to develop cognitive, social, and linguistic skills from an early age.
School Inclusion Programmes	Emphasizes inclusive classrooms, **training for teachers in special education techniques**, and **availability of resource persons** in schools.
Multilingual & Flexible Learning	Encourages **learning in the mother tongue**, alternative communication methods like **Braille & Indian Sign Language (ISL)**, and personalized learning plans.
Integration of Technology	Promotes the use of **AI-powered assistive technology, digital books, and voice-based learning tools** for students with disabilities.
Teacher Training & Capacity Building	Mandates **special training modules** on handling diverse learning needs, **differentiated instruction**, and **inclusive pedagogy** for all teachers.
Scholarships & Financial Support	Expands **scholarships, free transportation, assistive devices, and disability-friendly infrastructure** to improve accessibility.
Flexible Assessment & Evaluation	Offers alternative assessment methods like **oral exams, extra time, and adaptive question formats** for students with disabilities.
Barrier-Free Infrastructure	Enforces **ramps, accessible restrooms, assistive tech labs, and sensory-friendly learning environments** in all schools.

◎ Impact of NEP 2020 on Special Education & Inclusive Learning

1 Universal Access to Quality Education 📖

- **NEP 2020 prioritizes education for all** by removing barriers for students with disabilities through **accessible infrastructure, specialized teaching aids, and financial support.**
- **Schools must adopt inclusive curricula** tailored to different disabilities, ensuring holistic learning experiences.

2 Teacher Training & Curriculum Reform 🧑‍🏫📕

- **Mandatory special education training** for all teachers under the **National Council for Teacher Education (NCTE)** guidelines.
- **Emphasis on competency-based learning** ensures that students with disabilities get customized learning plans and **experiential learning opportunities.**

3 Multidisciplinary Learning & Digital Inclusion 💻🎓

- **Technology-driven accessibility** through AI-based learning aids, audio books, **screen readers**, and **adaptive testing methods.**
- **Introduction of ISL (Indian Sign Language) as a subject** to promote communication accessibility.

4 Socio-Emotional & Vocational Support 🤍💼

- **Dedicated counseling & career guidance** for students with disabilities to help in higher education and employment.
- **Vocational training programs** designed to support PwDs in skill development and self-employment.

5 Collaboration Between Government & NGOs 🏛️🤍

- **Public-private partnerships (PPP) encouraged** to ensure accessibility in mainstream schools.
- **Increased collaboration with NGOs** for **awareness programs, specialized teacher training, and assistive technology distribution.**

📚 Exam-Oriented MCQs & PYQs

1 What is the primary goal of NEP 2020?
a) Increase privatization of education
b) Ensure holistic and inclusive education
c) Replace traditional education with only online learning
d) Focus only on higher education reforms
✅ **Answer: b) Ensure holistic and inclusive education**

2 How does NEP 2020 support students with disabilities?
a) By mandating inclusive classrooms and assistive technologies
b) By allowing special schools only for disabled students
c) By making home-schooling compulsory for disabled students
d) By excluding disabled students from mainstream education
✅ **Answer: a) By mandating inclusive classrooms and assistive technologies**

3 Which provision of NEP 2020 promotes digital inclusion for students with disabilities?
a) Mandatory e-learning for all students
b) AI-powered assistive technologies & digital books
c) Removing all written exams
d) Making computer science compulsory
✅ **Answer: b) AI-powered assistive technologies & digital books**

4 How does NEP 2020 address teacher training for inclusive education?
a) Special education training is optional for teachers
b) Teachers must undergo mandatory training in handling disabilities
c) Only private schools need to provide special education training
d) Teachers should only focus on academically gifted students
✅ **Answer: b) Teachers must undergo mandatory training in handling disabilities**

5 What is the role of Indian Sign Language (ISL) in NEP 2020?
a) ISL is removed from schools
b) ISL is included as a subject and promoted for accessibility
c) ISL is only for special schools
d) ISL is mandatory for all students
✅ **Answer: b) ISL is included as a subject and promoted for accessibility**

🏛️ *The Rehabilitation Council of India (RCI) Act, 1992*

📝 What is the RCI Act, 1992?

The **Rehabilitation Council of India (RCI) Act, 1992** is a significant legislation designed to regulate the **education, training, and professional standards** for rehabilitation and special education services in India. The act ensures that **only certified professionals** provide rehabilitation services, enhancing the quality of support for **Persons with Disabilities (PwDs)**.

◆ **Enacted in:** 1992
◆ **Amendment:** Expanded in 2000 to include vocational training, employment, and rehabilitation services.
◆ **Administered by:** Ministry of Social Justice & Empowerment

---

📊 Key Features of the RCI Act, 1992

Feature	Details
Regulation of Rehabilitation Services 🏢	Ensures that only certified professionals provide rehabilitation services.
Standardized Special Education Training 🎓	Establishes curriculum guidelines and accreditation for institutions offering special education programs.
Mandatory Registration 🆔	Requires all professionals and training institutions to register with RCI before providing services.
Inspection & Monitoring 🔍	RCI has the power to inspect institutions and revoke licenses for non-compliance.
Expansion of Services ⚪	Encourages rehabilitation outreach in rural and underdeveloped areas.
Code of Conduct for Professionals ⚖️	Sets ethical guidelines and disciplinary actions for rehabilitation professionals.
Promotion of Research & Development 📖	Supports innovation and research in the field of special education and rehabilitation.

🎯 How Does the RCI Act Benefit Special Education?

Impact Area	Key Benefits
Strengthening Rehabilitation Services 🏢	Ensures better-trained professionals, reducing dependency on unqualified individuals.

Recognition of Special Education as a Profession 🎓 — Gives credibility and career growth opportunities to special educators.

Regulation of Training Institutions 🏫 — Helps maintain uniform standards and quality in special education programs.

Skill Development & Vocational Training 🧑 — Encourages PwDs to gain employment through structured skill-based programs.

Expanding Services to Rural Areas ⚫ — Ensures rehabilitation centers are accessible in remote regions.

📚 Exam-Focused MCQs & PYQs

1 What is the main objective of the RCI Act, 1992?
a) To improve healthcare services for PwDs
b) To regulate rehabilitation education and services
c) To promote general education in India
d) To fund special schools
☑ **Answer: b) To regulate rehabilitation education and services**

2 When was the RCI Act amended to expand its coverage?
a) 1995
b) 2000
c) 2016
d) 2020
☑ **Answer: b) 2000**

3 Who oversees the implementation of the RCI Act?
a) Ministry of Education
b) Ministry of Health and Family Welfare
c) Ministry of Social Justice & Empowerment
d) Ministry of Skill Development
☑ **Answer: c) Ministry of Social Justice & Empowerment**

4 Why is registration with RCI mandatory?
a) To control the employment of rehabilitation professionals
b) To ensure that only qualified individuals provide rehabilitation services
c) To provide financial aid to special educators
d) To limit the number of professionals in this field
☑ **Answer: b) To ensure that only qualified individuals provide rehabilitation services**

5 **How does the RCI Act help in rural areas?**
a) By setting up exclusive rehabilitation centers in cities
b) By limiting services to government hospitals
c) By promoting outreach and special education programs in remote areas
d) By restricting training institutions to government-run schools
✅ **Answer: c) By promoting outreach and special education programs in remote areas**

📚 *Sarva Shiksha Abhiyan (SSA) & Samagra Shiksha Abhiyan*

Education plays a **pivotal role** in shaping a nation's future. To ensure **equitable and quality learning opportunities**, the Indian government introduced **Sarva Shiksha Abhiyan (SSA)**, which later evolved into **Samagra Shiksha Abhiyan (SSA)**, enhancing educational accessibility, **modernization**, and **holistic development**.

🔘 Evolution of SSA to Samagra Shiksha Abhiyan

The journey of education reform in India has witnessed significant **transformations** over the years. The **Sarva Shiksha Abhiyan (SSA)** was launched in **2001** as a flagship program to ensure **universal elementary education**. With the implementation of the **Right to Education (RTE) Act, 2009**, SSA played a crucial role in making education **free and compulsory** for children aged **6-14 years**.

However, with the changing educational landscape and the need for **comprehensive school education**, the government introduced **Samagra Shiksha Abhiyan** in **2018**, integrating SSA with **Rashtriya Madhyamik Shiksha Abhiyan (RMSA)** and **Teacher Education (TE)**. This holistic approach aimed at **bridging learning gaps, promoting digital education, and strengthening teacher training**.

😊 Overview of SSA & Samagra Shiksha Abhiyan

📌 Scheme	📝 Description
Sarva Shiksha Abhiyan (SSA) ⬣	Initiated in **2001**, SSA aimed at achieving **universal elementary education**, ensuring **free and compulsory schooling** for children aged **6-14 years**, aligned with the **Right to Education (RTE) Act, 2009**.

| Samagra Shiksha Abhiyan | Launched in **2018**, this initiative integrated **pre-primary to senior secondary education**, merging SSA, RMSA (Rashtriya Madhyamik Shiksha Abhiyan), and TE (Teacher Education) for a **comprehensive learning framework**. |

🔍 Core Aspects of SSA & Samagra Shiksha Abhiyan

📌 Component	Sarva Shiksha Abhiyan (SSA)	Samagra Shiksha Abhiyan
Vision	Universalizing elementary education	A unified approach covering **pre-primary to 12th grade**
Target Group	Children aged 6-14 years	Children from **pre-school to senior secondary level**
Teacher Empowerment	Training programs for primary school educators	Strengthens **teacher recruitment, capacity-building & pedagogy**
Digital Integration	Basic ICT interventions	**Emphasis on smart classrooms, e-learning modules & ICT-driven education**
Mid-Day Meal	Free meals for elementary students	Expanded coverage for **nutritional support & well-being**
Infrastructure Expansion	Establishment of primary schools	Development of **libraries, science labs, and vocational skill hubs**
Inclusive Education	Special learning aids for disabled students	**Personalized assistive technologies & adaptive teaching methods**

📣 Key Features of Samagra Shiksha Abhiyan

◆ **Holistic Education Approach**: Covers pre-primary to higher secondary levels, ensuring **continuous and integrated learning**.

◆ **Digital Learning Initiatives**: Promotes **smart classrooms, e-learning resources, and digital literacy programs**.

◆ **Empowering Teachers**: Regular training programs, workshops, and **capacity-building initiatives** to enhance teaching effectiveness.

◆ **Special Focus on Girls' Education**: Financial assistance, scholarships, and **gender-sensitive learning environments**.

◆ **Support for Children with Disabilities**: Use of **assistive devices, specialized curriculum, and trained educators**.

◆ **Vocational Training**: Integration of **skill-based courses** to prepare students for employment opportunities.

✳ Transformational Impact of SSA & Samagra Shiksha Abhiyan

☑ **Higher Enrollment Rates** 🗹 – Increased participation, particularly among **girls and disadvantaged groups**.

☑ **Enhanced Literacy Levels** 📚 – Strengthened foundational literacy and numeracy skills.

☑ **Dropout Prevention Measures** 📉 – Financial assistance, scholarships, and flexible learning options.

☑ **Upgraded Learning Spaces** 🏫 – Smart classrooms, digital resources, and modern infrastructure.

☑ **Special Focus on Differently-Abled Students** 👨 🦽 – Adoption of inclusive teaching strategies and **assistive learning devices**.

📚 Exam-Oriented MCQs & PYQs

1 **In which year was Sarva Shiksha Abhiyan (SSA) launched?**
a) 1995
b) 2001
c) 2005
d) 2010
☑ **Answer: b) 2001**

2 **What is the primary focus of SSA?**
a) Universal higher education
b) Digital education for all
c) Universal elementary education (UEE)
d) Vocational training
☑ **Answer: c) Universal elementary education (UEE)**

3 **Which initiative merged SSA, RMSA, and TE?**
a) Mid-Day Meal Scheme
b) National Digital Learning Mission
c) Samagra Shiksha Abhiyan
d) National Education Program
☑ **Answer: c) Samagra Shiksha Abhiyan**

4 **What additional focus does Samagra Shiksha Abhiyan introduce?**
a) Restricting education to elementary level
b) Digital learning and inclusive education
c) Only primary education in rural areas
d) Mid-day meals for university students
☑ **Answer: b) Digital learning and inclusive education**

5 **Which scheme prioritizes teacher training and curriculum innovation?**
a) Sarva Shiksha Abhiyan
b) Samagra Shiksha Abhiyan
c) Pradhan Mantri Vidya Yojana
d) Digital India Learning Initiative
☑ **Answer: b) Samagra Shiksha Abhiyan**

📚 *Integrated Education for Disabled Children (IEDC) & Inclusive Education For Disabled at Secondary Stage (IEDSS)*

⚪ Understanding Inclusive Education

Education is a **fundamental right** for every child, including those with disabilities. Over the years, India has taken significant steps to **promote inclusive education**, ensuring that children with disabilities receive equal opportunities in mainstream schools. Two key government initiatives, **Integrated Education for Disabled Children (IEDC)** and **Inclusive Education for Disabled at Secondary Stage (IEDSS)**, have played a crucial role in shaping inclusive learning environments.

📌 Integrated Education for Disabled Children (IEDC)

😊 What is IEDC?

Launched in **1974**, the **Integrated Education for Disabled Children (IEDC)** scheme aimed at **mainstreaming children with disabilities** by integrating them into regular schools. It provided **financial assistance** for infrastructure, special educators, and learning aids to support students with disabilities.

◆ Key Features of IEDC

✓ **Mainstream Education** – Encouraged disabled students to study in regular schools.
✓ **Financial Support** – Provided scholarships, books, and school uniforms to disabled children.

✓ **Special Training for Teachers** – Focused on training regular teachers in special education methods.
✓ **Use of Assistive Devices** – Introduced hearing aids, Braille books, and mobility equipment for students.
✓ **Counseling & Awareness** – Conducted awareness programs for parents and teachers.

📊 Impact of IEDC

- **Increased Enrollment** – More children with disabilities started attending mainstream schools.
- **Reduction in Dropout Rates** – Students received **learning support and financial aid**, reducing early dropouts.
- **Foundation for Future Policies** – IEDC laid the groundwork for later inclusive education policies.

📌 Inclusive Education For Disabled at Secondary Stage (IEDSS)

😊 What is IEDSS?

The **Inclusive Education for Disabled at Secondary Stage (IEDSS)** scheme was launched in **2009** to extend inclusive education to **secondary school students (classes IX-XII)**. It replaced the IEDC scheme, focusing on **supporting disabled students beyond primary education**.

◆ Key Features of IEDSS

✓ **Education Beyond Primary Level** – Ensured disabled students continue education in high school.
✓ **Comprehensive Financial Assistance** – Funded **tuition fees, transport, books, hostel facilities, and scholarships**.
✓ **Advanced Assistive Technology** – Provided **speech therapy, physiotherapy, and adapted learning materials**.
✓ **Special Educators & Resource Centers** – Emphasized **individualized learning plans** for students.
✓ **Vocational Training & Skill Development** – Focused on job-oriented education for disabled youth.
✓ **Barrier-Free Environment** – Schools were modified with **ramps, accessible toilets, and customized furniture**.

📊 Impact of IEDSS

- **Improved Secondary Education Access** – More disabled students transitioned from primary to high school.

- **Enhanced Employment Opportunities** – Vocational education prepared students for future careers.
- **Empowerment of Students with Disabilities** – Gave them the confidence to pursue higher education and careers.

Comparison: IEDC vs. IEDSS

Feature	IEDC (1974)	IEDSS (2009)
Target Group	Children with disabilities in **primary schools**	Students with disabilities in **secondary schools**
Scope	Integration into regular schools	**Full inclusion and support** in secondary education
Financial Aid	Books, uniforms, basic learning materials	Tuition fees, transportation, hostel stay, and scholarships
Teacher Training	Basic training for primary school teachers	**Advanced training** and specialized educators
Assistive Technology	Basic learning aids	**Advanced assistive devices** (Braille tech, speech therapy)
Focus Areas	Early education and social integration	Career readiness, **vocational training, and skill development**

Challenges & Future Scope

Challenges in Implementing Inclusive Education

- **Lack of Trained Teachers** – Many schools still lack special educators.
- **Insufficient Infrastructure** – Not all schools have ramps, assistive devices, or resource rooms.
- **Social Stigma** – Some communities still resist the inclusion of disabled children in regular schools.
- **Limited Awareness** – Parents and teachers may not fully understand the benefits of inclusive education.

🚀 Future Steps to Improve Inclusive Education

√ **More Special Educators** – Mandatory teacher training programs for inclusive education.
√ **Digital & Assistive Technology** – Use of **AI-powered tools, audiobooks, and speech recognition** software.
√ **Stronger Government Policies** – Stricter implementation of **RPWD Act, 2016**, to enforce accessibility in schools.
√ **Community Awareness Programs** – Campaigns to educate parents and teachers about **inclusive education benefits**.

📝 Exam-Oriented MCQs & PYQs

1 When was the Integrated Education for Disabled Children (IEDC) scheme launched?
a) 1986
b) 1995
c) 1974
d) 2001
✓ **Answer: c) 1974**

2 What was the primary objective of the IEDC scheme?
a) To provide vocational education to disabled students
b) To integrate disabled children into regular schools
c) To provide only home-based education for disabled students
d) To offer separate schools for disabled students
✓ **Answer: b) To integrate disabled children into regular schools**

3 In which year was the Inclusive Education for Disabled at Secondary Stage (IEDSS) scheme introduced?
a) 2001
b) 2005
c) 2009
d) 2012
✓ **Answer: c) 2009**

4 What is the main difference between IEDC and IEDSS?
a) IEDC is for primary education, IEDSS is for secondary education
b) IEDSS focuses only on vocational training
c) IEDC provides hostel facilities, IEDSS does not
d) IEDC is for college-level students
✓ **Answer: a) IEDC is for primary education, IEDSS is for secondary education**

5 What additional support does IEDSS provide compared to IEDC?
a) Advanced assistive technology

https://www.specialeducationnotes.in

b) Vocational training
c) Financial support for tuition, transport, and hostel stay
d) All of the above
☑ **Answer: d) All of the above**

📑 *United Nations Convention on the Rights of Persons with Disabilities (UNCRPD)*

🔘 A Global Commitment to Disability Rights

The **United Nations Convention on the Rights of Persons with Disabilities (UNCRPD)** is a landmark international treaty adopted in **2006** to promote and protect the **rights and dignity of persons with disabilities** worldwide. India ratified it in **2007**, committing the country to ensuring **full inclusion and equal opportunities** for persons with disabilities.

📌 Key Objectives of UNCRPD

◆ **Human Rights Protection** – Ensuring equal rights and opportunities for all persons with disabilities.
◆ **Non-Discrimination** – Eliminating barriers in education, employment, and social participation.
◆ **Accessibility Enhancement** – Making public spaces, transport, and digital platforms disabled-friendly.
◆ **Empowerment & Inclusion** – Promoting independent living and full social participation.
◆ **Global Collaboration** – Encouraging countries to work together for disability rights.

📌 Core Principles of UNCRPD

◆ **Respect for Inherent Dignity** – Treating individuals with disabilities as full members of society.
◆ **Full & Effective Participation** – Encouraging disabled persons to engage in all aspects of life.
◆ **Equality of Opportunity** – Guaranteeing fair access to education, employment, and healthcare.
◆ **Accessibility** – Removing physical, digital, and communication barriers.
◆ **Gender Equality** – Recognizing the rights and needs of women with disabilities.
◆ **Respect for Children with Disabilities** – Providing them with special protection and support.
◆ **Independent Living** – Ensuring self-reliance and personal decision-making.

---

     https://www.specialeducationnotes.in

📌 India's Implementation of UNCRPD

1 Rights of Persons with Disabilities (RPWD) Act, 2016

- Expanded the disability categories from **7 to 21**.
- Mandated **5% reservation in government jobs**.
- Ensured **education, healthcare, and employment rights**.

2 Accessible India Campaign (Sugamya Bharat Abhiyan)

- Aimed at **making public spaces, transport, and ICT accessible**.
- Focused on **creating a barrier-free environment**.

3 Inclusive Education Policies

- **National Education Policy (NEP) 2020** supports inclusive learning.
- **Samagra Shiksha Abhiyan** integrates disabled children into mainstream schools.

4 Skill Development & Employment Initiatives

- **National Action Plan for Skill Development** provides job training.
- Encourages **entrepreneurship & economic empowerment**.

💥 Challenges in Implementing UNCRPD in India

✖ **Lack of Awareness** – Many disabled individuals are unaware of their rights.
✖ **Infrastructural Barriers** – Accessibility in schools, workplaces, and public spaces remains a challenge.
✖ **Slow Policy Implementation** – Many government initiatives face delays.
✖ **Employment Gaps** – Despite reservations, hiring remains low for disabled individuals.

🚀 Future Strategies for Better Implementation

☑ **Stronger Law Enforcement** – Monitoring the **RPWD Act** effectively.
☑ **Improved Accessibility** – Expanding **inclusive infrastructure & digital access**.
☑ **Public Awareness Campaigns** – Spreading knowledge on disability rights.
☑ **Enhanced Special Education Support** – Increasing funding for education & healthcare.

📝 Exam-Oriented MCQs & PYQs

1 When was the UNCRPD adopted by the United Nations?
a) 2000
b) 2006
c) 2010
d) 2016
✓ **Answer: b) 2006**

2 In which year did India ratify the UNCRPD?
a) 2006
b) 2007
c) 2009
d) 2012
✓ **Answer: b) 2007**

3 Which Indian law was introduced to align with UNCRPD principles?
a) The Rehabilitation Council of India Act, 1992
b) The Rights of Persons with Disabilities Act, 2016
c) The Sarva Shiksha Abhiyan Act
d) The Mental Health Act, 2017
✓ **Answer: b) The Rights of Persons with Disabilities Act, 2016**

4 What is the core principle of UNCRPD?
a) Separate education for disabled persons
b) Full inclusion and accessibility for all
c) Financial assistance only
d) Limiting job opportunities for persons with disabilities
✓ **Answer: b) Full inclusion and accessibility for all**

5 What does the Accessible India Campaign focus on?
a) Employment of disabled individuals
b) Building an inclusive financial system
c) Improving physical and digital accessibility
d) Reserving seats in government institutions
✓ **Answer: c) Improving physical and digital accessibility**

📚 *Acts, Organizations & Institutions Related to Special Education*

📝 *Important Acts Related to Special Education*

1 Rights of Persons with Disabilities (RPWD) Act, 2016

- Expands the recognized disabilities from **7 to 21 categories**.
- Ensures **equal opportunities in education, employment, and social participation**.
- Mandates **5% reservation in higher education institutions & government jobs**.

2 Rehabilitation Council of India (RCI) Act, 1992

- Regulates and standardizes **training programs for special educators & rehabilitation professionals**.
- Maintains a **central registry of trained rehabilitation professionals**.
- Ensures **quality standards in special education institutions**.

3 National Trust Act, 1999

- Focuses on **empowering persons with autism, cerebral palsy, mental retardation, and multiple disabilities**.
- Provides **legal guardianship and financial support** to affected families.
- Implements **schemes for independent living and employment**.

4 The Right to Education (RTE) Act, 2009

- Guarantees **free and compulsory education** for children aged **6-14 years**, including children with disabilities.
- Emphasizes **inclusive education and non-discrimination**.
- Mandates **barrier-free infrastructure in schools**.

5 Mental Healthcare Act, 2017

- Provides **rights-based protection** for individuals with mental illness.
- Focuses on **rehabilitation, de-stigmatization, and community integration**.
- Guarantees **affordable mental healthcare services**.

🏛️ *Major Organizations Working in Special Education*

1 Rehabilitation Council of India (RCI)

- Regulates **special education programs and teacher training**.
- Maintains a **national database of rehabilitation professionals**.
- Conducts research and policy development in special education.

2 National Institute for Empowerment of Persons with Visual Disabilities (NIEPVD)

- Develops **braille education and assistive technology**.
- Provides **vocational training for the visually impaired**.
- Promotes **inclusive education strategies**.

3 National Institute for the Empowerment of Persons with Intellectual Disabilities (NIEPID)

- Works on **early intervention and skill development** for individuals with intellectual disabilities.
- Offers **teacher training programs in special education**.
- Conducts **awareness programs and community outreach**.

4 National Institute for Locomotor Disabilities (NILD)

- Develops **prosthetic and assistive devices**.
- Focuses on **mobility rehabilitation and therapy**.
- Provides **technical training to special educators and therapists**.

5 Ali Yavar Jung National Institute of Speech and Hearing Disabilities (AYJNISHD)

- Provides **speech therapy and hearing aid services**.
- Trains special educators in **communication-based interventions**.
- Conducts **research on speech and language disorders**.

🏫 *Institutions Supporting Special Education in India*

1 National Council of Educational Research and Training (NCERT)

- Designs **inclusive education policies and curriculum**.
- Develops **special learning materials and assistive technology tools**.
- Trains teachers in **inclusive pedagogy**.

2 University Grants Commission (UGC)

- Promotes **higher education accessibility for students with disabilities**.
- Funds research on **special education methodologies**.
- Provides **scholarships and financial aid** for disabled students.

3 Indian Sign Language Research and Training Centre (ISLRTC)

- Develops **Indian Sign Language (ISL) curriculum**.
- Trains teachers in **sign language interpretation**.
- Conducts **awareness campaigns for hearing-impaired education**.

4 Central Institute of Educational Technology (CIET)

- Develops **digital learning resources for children with disabilities**.
- Works on **accessible e-learning platforms**.
- Conducts research on **assistive technology in education**.

🎯 Conclusion

India has a well-defined framework for **special education** through various **laws, organizations, and institutions**. However, **stronger implementation, awareness campaigns, and technological advancements** are needed to make education truly **inclusive and accessible** for all.

🚀 *Schemes Related to Special Education (Central & State Govt.)*

Education is a fundamental right, and ensuring inclusive education for children with disabilities is a priority. The Indian government, both at the **central** and **state** levels, has introduced several schemes to support children with special needs. Let's explore some key initiatives! 🎯

1 Sarva Shiksha Abhiyan (SSA) – Education for All

- Ensures **free and compulsory education** for all children, including those with disabilities.
- Focuses on **barrier-free schools, home-based learning, and inclusive classrooms**.
- Provides **free assistive devices, study materials, and financial aid** to ensure accessibility.

2 Samagra Shiksha Abhiyan (SSA) – Holistic Learning Approach

- Covers **education from pre-primary to higher secondary** for children with disabilities.
- Trains **teachers and special educators** to support inclusive learning.
- Encourages **ICT-based learning** and school infrastructure improvements.

3 Deendayal Disabled Rehabilitation Scheme (DDRS) – Empowering NGOs

- Supports **NGOs working in special education and rehabilitation**.
- Funds **vocational training, therapy centers, and special schools**.
- Promotes **community-based rehabilitation and employment opportunities**.

4 Scholarship Schemes for Disabled Students – Promoting Higher Education

- **National Fellowship for Persons with Disabilities (RGMF)** – Assists students in **higher studies**.
- **Pre-Matric & Post-Matric Scholarships** – Aims at **reducing dropout rates**.
- **Top Class Education for Students with Disabilities** – Encourages **higher education in prestigious institutions**.

5 Accessible India Campaign (Sugamya Bharat Abhiyan) – Building an Inclusive India

- Aims at making **public spaces, transport, and schools disability-friendly**.
- Provides **assistive technology and digital accessibility tools**.
- Ensures **modern, inclusive school infrastructure**.

🏛 *State Govt. Initiatives*

1 Tamil Nadu – CM's Comprehensive Health Insurance Scheme (CMCHIS)

- Offers **free medical treatment and therapy** for children with disabilities.

- Covers **special education and rehabilitation programs**.

2 Maharashtra – Pune Model for Inclusive Education

- Establishes **resource centers** to provide specialized support in mainstream schools.
- Trains **special educators** and provides **assistive devices**.

3 Kerala – Inclusive Education for the Disabled at Secondary Stage (IEDSS)

- Provides **free education, transport, and assistive technology**.
- Offers **vocational training and life skills programs**.

4 Uttar Pradesh – Divyangjan Shiksha Samman Yojana

- Grants **scholarships and financial incentives** to students with disabilities.
- Enhances **access to special schools and transport facilities**.

5 West Bengal – Manabik Pension Scheme

- Provides **financial assistance** to individuals with disabilities.
- Supports **community-based disability programs and awareness campaigns**.

🔍 Conclusion – Moving Towards True Inclusion

India has made significant progress in **promoting inclusive education** through various **government schemes**. However, the success of these initiatives depends on **effective implementation, continuous monitoring, and public awareness**. A truly **inclusive society** is one where **every child, regardless of ability, has access to quality education and opportunities for growth**. 🔑

4 Special Psychology & Psychological Support

🧩 1. Meaning of Inclusive Education

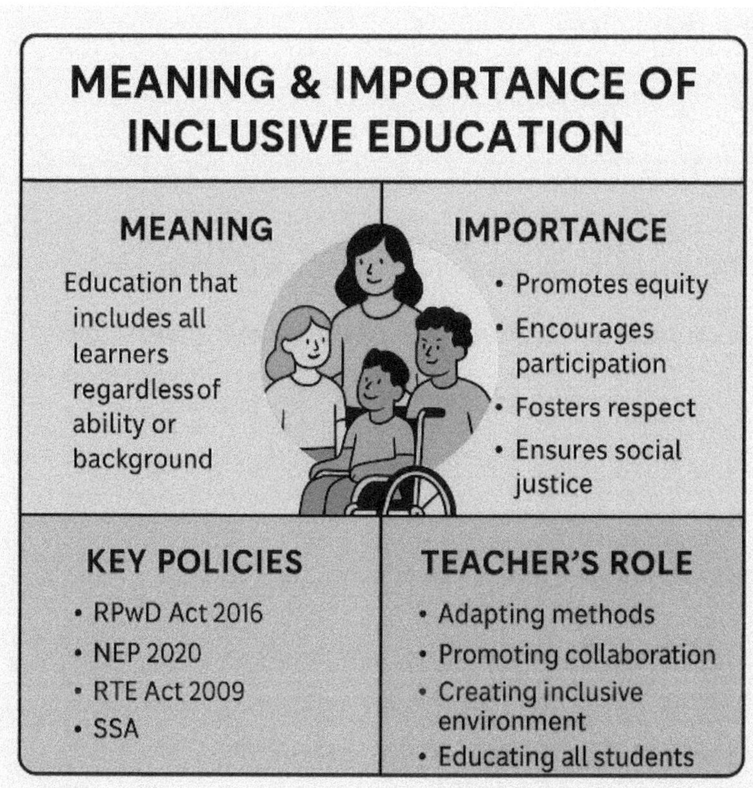

Inclusive Education is a **philosophy and practice** that ensures all children — regardless of their **ability, disability, socio-economic background, language, gender, or caste** — learn **together in the same classroom**.

☑ It is based on the principle of **equity, access, participation, and success** for every learner.

🔍 Definitions:

Scholar / Source	Definition
UNESCO (2009)	"Inclusive Education is a process of addressing and responding to the diversity of needs of all learners by increasing participation in learning, cultures, and communities."
NCF 2005	"Inclusion is about embracing all. It is about creating a world that values diversity and supports learning for all."

❇ Importance of Inclusive Education

No.	Importance
1.	**Promotes Equality & Social Justice** – All learners get equal opportunities regardless of differences.
2.	**Reduces Discrimination** – Children grow up respecting diversity and differences.
3.	**Improves Academic & Social Outcomes** – Collaborative learning helps all students.
4.	**Prepares for Real World** – Reflects a diverse society and teaches adaptability.
5.	**Strengthens Community** – Parents, teachers, and peers work together to support every child.
6.	**Empowers Children with Special Needs** – Builds confidence and reduces marginalisation.

📊 Key Differences: Inclusive vs Exclusive Education

Feature	Exclusive Education	Inclusive Education
Setting	Separate schools for special needs	Same classroom for all
Focus	Disability-focused	Diversity-focused
Goal	Specialised learning	Equal participation
Teacher Role	Specialist only	Collaborative & adaptive

🏛 Policies Supporting Inclusive Education in India

Policy / Programme	Highlights
RPwD Act, 2016	Mandates inclusive education in neighbourhood schools
NEP 2020	Emphasizes equitable and inclusive education for all
Sarva Shiksha Abhiyan (SSA)	Promotes education of children with special needs

Right to Education Act, 2009	Ensures free and compulsory education to all 6–14-year-olds including CWSN

🎓 Role of Teachers in Inclusive Education

- Adapting **curriculum and teaching methods**

- Using **differentiated instruction**

- Providing **peer support and buddy systems**

- Ensuring a **barrier-free environment**

- Developing **positive attitude and awareness** among students

💬 PYQs (Previous Year Questions)

📌 DSSSB 2021:

Q: What is the main aim of Inclusive Education?
A) To teach only children with disabilities
B) To educate all children together irrespective of their abilities
C) To give special schools more importance
D) None of the above
☑ **Answer: B**

📌 KVS 2018:

Q: According to RTE Act, children with special needs should be—
A) Sent to special schools
B) Given home-based education only
C) Included in regular schools
D) Taught only by special educators
☑ **Answer: C**

📝 Practice MCQs

1. Inclusive education mainly focuses on:
   A) Special curriculum
   B) Equal participation of all learners
   C) Individualised learning only
   D) Restricting learners with disabilities
   ☑ **Answer:** B

2. Which policy mandates inclusive education in India?
   A) NEP 1986
   B) RPwD Act, 2016
   C) UGC Act
   D) SSA 2001
   ☑ **Answer:** B

3. Inclusion in classrooms promotes:
   A) Competition
   B) Discrimination
   C) Collaboration and respect
   D) Isolation
   ☑ **Answer:** C

📌 Summary Chart: Inclusive Education at a Glance

Aspect	Description
Meaning	Education that includes all learners regardless of ability or background
Importance	Promotes equity, participation, respect, and social justice
Key Policies	RPwD Act 2016, NEP 2020, RTE Act 2009, SSA
Teacher's Role	Adapting methods, promoting collaboration, creating inclusive environment

🧩 2. Barriers to Inclusion & Strategies to Overcome Them 🚧

🚧 What Are Barriers to Inclusion?

Imagine trying to enter a room that has no ramp, the door is locked, and nobody is there to help —
that's how a child with special needs can feel in a **non-inclusive environment**.

🔎 **Barriers to Inclusion** are **obstacles** (physical, social, attitudinal, policy-based) that
prevent full participation of diverse learners in mainstream classrooms.

⚙️ Types of Barriers to Inclusion

Let's break this down in a fun and simple table 👇

🧩 Type of Barrier	🚫 Examples
Physical	No ramps, inaccessible toilets, narrow doorways
Attitudinal	Teachers' low expectations, bullying, social stigma
Curricular	Rigid curriculum, no accommodations for diverse needs
Policy/Administrative	Lack of inclusive policies, unclear guidelines
Teacher-related	No training, fear of handling special needs
Parental/Community	Lack of awareness, resistance to inclusion

🧰 Strategies to Overcome Barriers (With Examples!)

🛠️ Strategy	☑️ What It Does
Universal Design for Learning (UDL)	Designs lessons that work for *everyone*, not just "average" students
Teacher Training & Sensitization	Equips teachers with skills & empathy
Peer Support Programs	Encourages inclusive friendship & support
Infrastructure Modification	Adds ramps, tactile paths, accessible toilets

Flexible Curriculum	Allows multiple modes of expression & assessment
Involvement of Parents/Community	Builds support system beyond the classroom
Use of ICT & Assistive Technology	Helps learners with disabilities to participate fully

---

🎓 Real-life Example:

Rita, a 9-year-old with visual impairment, was excluded from reading activities. After her school introduced **Braille materials and a buddy reader system**, she became an active participant in class.

✨ That's inclusion in action!

📌 Chart: Barriers vs Solutions

🚩 Barrier Type	🔧 Strategy to Overcome
Physical	Ramps, tactile flooring, elevators
Attitudinal	Awareness programs, empathy training
Curricular	UDL, differentiated instruction
Teacher Training	In-service workshops, inclusive education modules
Policy	Implementation of RPwD Act, NEP 2020 guidelines

🪨 PYQs (Previous Year Questions)

📌 CTET 2020:

Q: Which of the following is an attitudinal barrier to inclusion?
A) Lack of ramps

B) Teachers' negative beliefs about disabled children
C) No Braille books
D) Unclear school rules
☑ **Answer:** B

📌 DSSSB 2019:

Q: What is an effective strategy to promote inclusion in schools?
A) Use of competitive grading
B) Uniform curriculum for all
C) Peer tutoring and group activities
D) Segregation based on ability
☑ **Answer:** C

🖐 Practice MCQs

1. Which of the following is a **curricular barrier** to inclusion?
   A) Inaccessible toilets
   B) Rigid syllabus without accommodations
   C) Lack of ramps
   D) Parental resistance
   ☑ **Answer:** B

2. **Universal Design for Learning (UDL)** aims to:
   A) Create separate content for disabled learners
   B) Restrict access to complex subjects
   C) Design flexible learning for all students
   D) Replace mainstream curriculum
   ☑ **Answer:** C

3. Teacher's lack of training is considered a:
   A) Physical barrier
   B) Personal choice
   C) Policy barrier
   D) Teacher-related barrier
   ☑ **Answer:** D

◎ Summary in 1 Minute (Quick Recap)

◆ *Inclusion fails* when barriers like infrastructure gaps, rigid curriculum, untrained teachers, and social stigma are not addressed.
◆ The solution lies in **training, technology, flexibility**, and **community participation**.
◆ Think: *More ramps. Less rejection. More love. Less labels.*

🧩 3. Universal Design for Learning (UDL) & Its Implementation

💭 What is Universal Design for Learning (UDL)?

Imagine designing a classroom **where every student can learn – no matter how they learn best**. That's the magic of UDL.

> ✳️ **UDL is a flexible educational approach** that aims to create learning environments that accommodate all learners, regardless of their abilities or backgrounds.

🔍 Official Definition (CAST):

"Universal Design for Learning is a framework to improve and optimize teaching and learning for all people based on scientific insights into how humans learn."

◎ The 3 Principles of UDL

(aka the "golden triangle" of inclusive teaching)

Principle	Focus	Practical Example
1. Multiple Means of Representation	*The "what" of learning*	Use text, audio, video, Braille, visuals
2. Multiple Means of Action & Expression	*The "how" of learning*	Let students write, draw, act, or type responses
3. Multiple Means of Engagement	*The "why" of learning*	Use games, group work, storytelling to boost interest

🎨 Visual learners? Use diagrams.
🎧 Audio learners? Use podcasts.

Kinesthetic learners? Use role-play.

UDL says: "One size doesn't fit all!"

🧩 Why is UDL Important?

Benefit	How it Helps
Inclusive	Meets diverse learning needs in one classroom
Flexible	Adapts content for every type of learner
Reduces Barriers	Avoids the need for "special" accommodations later
Boosts Motivation	Students learn in their comfort zone
Improves Learning Outcomes	Personalized paths lead to better results

---

🛠️ UDL Implementation in the Classroom

Here's a table showing practical ways teachers can implement UDL 👇

UDL Principle	Implementation Strategy
Representation	Use images, infographics, hands-on materials, subtitles, mind maps
Action & Expression	Let students choose how to demonstrate learning – posters, videos, presentations
Engagement	Provide choices, encourage curiosity, use tech tools, include personal goals

💡 Pro Tip: Use **assistive technologies** like screen readers, speech-to-text, and interactive whiteboards to support learners with disabilities.

📊 UDL at a Glance – Visual Summary Chart

⚠ Principle	💡 Examples
Representation	Visual aids, Braille, sign language
Expression	Oral presentations, writing, drawing
Engagement	Games, rewards, storytelling, interest surveys

📜 Government & Policy Support

Policy	UDL Reference
NEP 2020	Emphasizes flexibility & learner-centric approaches
RPwD Act 2016	Promotes accessible education through inclusive design
NCF 2005 & 2023	Encourages diverse learning styles and curriculum adaptation

💭 Previous Year Questions (PYQs)

📌 CTET 2021:

Q: Universal Design for Learning promotes:
A) Standardized teaching for all
B) Same instructional method
C) Flexible methods to support diverse learners
D) Segregation of students based on ability
☑ **Answer:** C

📌 DSSSB 2020:

Q: Which is *not* a principle of UDL?
A) Multiple means of representation
B) Multiple means of memorization
C) Multiple means of expression

D) Multiple means of engagement

☑ **Answer:** B

🖐 Practice MCQs

1. Which of the following aligns with UDL principles?
   A) One textbook for all
   B) Teaching only through lecture
   C) Providing visual, audio, and kinesthetic content
   D) Assigning only written tests
   ☑ **Answer:** C

2. UDL ensures—
   A) Homogeneous classrooms
   B) Uniform instruction
   C) Equal access and flexible learning
   D) Separate special education schools
   ☑ **Answer:** C

3. A UDL classroom encourages—
   A) Copy-paste learning
   B) Learner choice and motivation
   C) Memorization only
   D) Only traditional exams
   ☑ **Answer:** B

💬 Fun Analogy: UDL is like a Buffet! 🍽

Just like a buffet lets people choose their food based on taste, diet, and need — **UDL lets learners choose how they access content and show what they know.**
🎯 It's fair, flexible, and deliciously effective!

4. Role of Regular Teachers & Special Educators in Inclusion

Introduction: Two Pillars of Inclusive Classrooms

In an inclusive setup, **both regular teachers and special educators work as a team** to support diverse learners — including those with disabilities, learning difficulties, or social disadvantages.

Think of it as:

- **Regular Teacher** = *Captain of the Class*
- **Special Educator** = *Co-pilot for Support & Adaptation*

Both roles are different but complementary.

Role of Regular Teachers in Inclusion

Regular teachers are like the **frontline warriors of inclusion**. Here's what they do:

Responsibility	Role
Creating Inclusive Environment	Foster acceptance, empathy, and collaboration among students
Flexible Teaching Methods	Use visuals, storytelling, group work, hands-on activities
Peer Support & Grouping	Arrange mixed-ability group tasks
Collaboration with Special Educators	Discuss IEPs, share progress, seek guidance
Monitoring Progress	Observe & assess children with diverse needs

Example: Ms. Ritu uses **visual aids, peer tutoring**, and allows **extra time** in tests for CWSN students in her regular class.

⬤ Role of Special Educators in Inclusion

Special educators are the **specialized support system** in inclusive education. Their job is to:

🛠 Function	🧩 Role
Designing IEPs (Individualized Education Plans)	Tailor goals & strategies for each child with special needs
Assessment & Screening	Identify specific learning needs early
Adaptation of Curriculum & Materials	Modify content and assessments
Training Teachers & Parents	Build capacity & awareness
Behavior Management	Support emotional and behavioral challenges
Use of Assistive Technology	Recommend and train on tools like screen readers, AAC devices, etc.

✏️ Example: Mr. Arvind, a special educator, helps adapt textbooks into **Braille** for a visually impaired student and trains the class teacher on inclusive techniques.

🐾 Collaboration Between the Two: Inclusion in Action!

🐾 Teamwork Element	🎊 Outcome
Regular + Special Educator plan lessons	Lessons reach all learning styles
Joint parent-teacher meetings	Builds trust and shared responsibility
Co-teaching models	One teaches, other assists or rotates
Shared progress tracking	Better understanding of student growth

💬 **Inclusion is not just about presence in the classroom — it's about participation.** This is only possible when both teachers work together.

📊 Quick Chart: Comparison of Roles

Feature / Task	Regular Teacher	Special Educator
Plans general lessons	✓	✗
Develops IEP	✗	✓
Conducts general assessments	✓	✗
Provides disability-specific support	✗	✓
Collaborates in team meetings	✓	✓
Handles behavior issues	✓	✓ (in complex cases)

📜 Government Guidelines Supporting These Roles

📔 Policy	📌 Role Highlight
NEP 2020	Training for regular teachers + integration of special educators
RPwD Act 2016	Mandates both types of teachers for inclusive education
Samagra Shiksha Abhiyan	Funds inclusive setups including resource rooms, training
NCF 2005 & 2023	Encourages team teaching and curriculum adaptation

🌥 PYQs (Previous Year Questions)

📌 CTET 2020:

Q: The role of a special educator in an inclusive classroom includes:
A) Teaching only mathematics
B) Identifying gifted students
C) Supporting children with disabilities through adaptations
D) Replacing the regular teacher
☑ **Answer:** C

📌 KVS 2018:

Q: Who is primarily responsible for creating a classroom environment that supports inclusion?
A) Special educator only
B) Principal
C) Regular teacher
D) Resource teacher
☑ **Answer:** C

✏ Practice MCQs

1. Regular teachers are responsible for—
   A) Creating IEPs
   B) Teaching in special schools
   C) Providing inclusive learning environments
   D) Diagnosing disabilities
   ☑ **Answer:** C

2. A special educator in an inclusive setup helps in—
   A) Designing mainstream syllabus
   B) Supporting individual learning needs of CWSN
   C) Conducting annual exams
   D) Supervising school buses
   ☑ **Answer:** B

3. Which of the following is a shared role between regular and special educators?
   A) Delivering medical treatment
   B) Curriculum policy-making
   C) Student progress monitoring
   D) Financial planning

✅ **Answer: C**

🎇 Summary: Two Halves of a Whole

A **regular teacher** brings in the curriculum.
A **special educator** brings in access for every child.
Together, they make **inclusive learning a reality** 🖤

🧩 5. Individualized Education Program (IEP) & Its Components

🎯 What is an IEP (Individualized Education Program)?

An **IEP** is a **customized educational plan** designed **for students with disabilities**, outlining their **unique learning goals, support services**, and **assessment methods**.

🔖 Mandated under laws like the **RPwD Act 2016 (India)** & **IDEA (USA)**, the IEP ensures that **Children With Special Needs (CWSN)** get **personalized support** within an inclusive setup.

🖼 Why Is IEP Important?

🎇 Benefit	🎯 Impact
Personalized Goals	Matches student's pace & potential
Targeted Support	Focuses on specific challenges
Clear Roles	Defines duties for teachers, therapists, parents
Progress Tracking	Enables timely review & intervention
Promotes Inclusion	Builds bridge between special & regular education

💬 Think of IEP as a **"Google Map" for a CWSN's learning journey** — showing the path, stops, and goals.

🗒️ Key Components of an IEP (With Chart)

🧩 Component	📌 Description
1. Present Level of Performance (PLOP)	Current academic, social, behavioral, and physical performance of the student
2. Annual Goals	Clear, measurable goals for the academic year
3. Short-term Objectives	Smaller steps to achieve annual goals
4. Special Education Services	Specific instruction, therapies, assistive devices needed
5. Participation in Regular Curriculum	Extent to which the child will be involved in the regular classroom
6. Accommodations & Modifications	Adjustments in teaching methods, materials, or assessment
7. Progress Monitoring	Tools & methods used to measure growth
8. Transition Planning *(for 14+ age)*	Prepares students for life after school (vocational skills, jobs, etc.)
9. Team Members & Signatures	Involves regular teacher, special educator, parents, therapist, principal, and the student (if appropriate)

📊 IEP Process Flowchart

```
Referral/Identification

        ↓

Evaluation (Cognitive, Social, Academic)

        ↓
```

```
IEP Team Formation
        ↓
IEP Meeting & Planning
        ↓
Implementation in Classroom
        ↓
Review & Revision (every 6–12 months)
```

💡 IEP is not a one-time document — it's a **dynamic plan** that grows with the child!

👥 Who Makes an IEP? (The IEP Team)

👤 Member	🎯 Role
Parents/Guardians	Share insights about the child at home
Regular Teacher	Provide classroom observations
Special Educator	Design accommodations, track progress
Therapists (Speech, OT, PT)	Suggest therapeutic goals
School Principal	Supervise IEP implementation
Student (when appropriate)	Shares own learning experiences

📜 Legal Backing of IEP in India

📕 Law	IEP Relevance
RPwD Act 2016	Mandates individualized support in inclusive setups
NEP 2020	Supports need-based, flexible learning plans

PYQs (Previous Year Questions)

CTET 2021:

Q: The main purpose of an IEP is to:
A) Ensure students are promoted
B) Provide uniform syllabus
C) Support CWSN with individualized plans
D) Maintain school records
☑ **Answer:** C

DSSSB 2019:

Q: Which of the following is *not* a component of an IEP?
A) Annual goals
B) Present level of performance
C) Family income details
D) Special education services
☑ **Answer:** C

Practice MCQs

1. Which of the following is included in an IEP?
   A) Sibling academic records
   B) Special education services for the child
   C) School holiday list
   D) Uniform size details
   ☑ **Answer:** B

2. The person responsible for implementing IEP in the classroom is—
   A) School clerk
   B) Regular teacher & special educator
   C) Parents only
   D) Sports teacher
   ☑ **Answer:** B

          https://www.specialeducationnotes.in

3. "Transition planning" in an IEP refers to:
   A) Shifting schools
   B) Preparing for exams
   C) Planning life after school for older CWSN
   D) Changing syllabus
   ✅ **Answer:** C

🌟 Real Example:

Rahul, a 10-year-old with dyslexia, had trouble with reading and writing. His IEP included goals like:

- Recognizing 50 new words in 3 months

- Using a text-to-speech app

- Allowing oral assessments
  ✅ Within 6 months, Rahul's reading improved, and his confidence soared!

🧩 6. Adaptations & Modifications in Curriculum & Teaching Methods

🎯 Introduction: Why Adapt or Modify?

Not all children learn the same way. Children with disabilities or diverse learning needs often require **changes in teaching methods or curriculum** so that they can learn **effectively and meaningfully**.

🌟 **Adaptation = Same Goal, Different Path**
🌟 **Modification = Adjusting the Goal Itself**

Definitions: Adaptations vs. Modifications

Term	Meaning	Example
Adaptation	Changes in **how** a student learns	Using audiobooks instead of printed text
Modification	Changes in **what** a student learns	Reducing the number of math problems from 10 to 5

→ **Adaptation** keeps the learning **goal same** but changes **presentation, tools, or response**
→ **Modification** changes the **learning expectations**

Types of Curriculum Adaptations

Type	Description	Example
Presentation	How information is given	Use large print, Braille, visuals, audio
Response	How students show what they know	Oral answers instead of writing
Timing/Scheduling	Time or structure changes	Extended test time, breaks
Environment	Changes to setting	Quiet corner for ADHD child
Curriculum Content	Simplifying topics	Use age-appropriate, functional content
Participation	Level of involvement	Use of buddy system in sports or activities

---

Teaching Method Adaptations for CWSN

Disability Type	Teaching Adaptation
Visual Impairment	Use audio materials, tactile graphics, Braille
Hearing Impairment	Use sign language, captions, visual cues

Autism	Use structured routines, visual schedules
Learning Disabilities (LD)	Use multisensory teaching, graphic organizers
Intellectual Disability	Break concepts into smaller steps, use repetition
ADHD	Provide movement breaks, keep instructions short

🔧 Common Classroom Adaptation Tools

Tool	Purpose
Graphic Organizers	Helps organize thoughts visually
Text-to-Speech Software	For reading difficulties
Fidget Tools	Helps students with sensory needs stay focused
Visual Timetables	Provides structure for neurodivergent learners
Simplified Worksheets	Reduces cognitive load for CWSN

📜 Legal & Policy Support in India

Policy / Act	Support for Adaptation
RPwD Act 2016	Ensures curriculum modifications for disabled students
NEP 2020	Promotes flexibility and inclusion in content delivery
NCF 2005 & 2023	Supports need-based and child-centric learning
Samagra Shiksha	Funds inclusive practices and resource materials

🎯 Real-Life Examples

🧩 *Example 1:* A student with a writing disability is allowed to type answers or use voice input in exams. *(Adaptation)*

🧩 *Example 2:* A student with an intellectual disability is given a life-skill-based math curriculum instead of algebra. *(Modification)*

> 💬 *Inclusive education is not about lowering standards; it's about leveling the playing field.*

💭 PYQs (Previous Year Questions)

📌 CTET 2021:

Q: Providing large print books to a visually impaired student is an example of—
A) Curriculum change
B) Teaching method
C) Adaptation
D) Modification
☑ **Answer:** C

📌 DSSSB 2020:

Q: Reducing the number of questions in a test for a child with a learning disability is an example of—
A) Evaluation
B) Modification
C) Accommodation
D) Testing technique
☑ **Answer:** B

👍 Practice MCQs

1. Changing the **way** a student responds to a task without changing the content is called—
   A) Modification
   B) Adaptation
   C) Exclusion
   D) Segregation
   ☑ **Answer:** B

2. A student is allowed to use a calculator in math due to disability. This is—
   A) Adaptation

B) Discrimination
C) Modification
D) Advantage
☑ **Answer:** A

3. Curriculum modifications are necessary when—
    A) Every student wants it
    B) A child cannot meet the standard learning outcomes
    C) Parents demand it
    D) Exam dates are approaching
    ☑ **Answer:** B

📊 Quick Comparison Table

Feature	Adaptation	Modification
Goal Remains Same?	☑ Yes	✖ No (Simplified)
Content Changed?	✖ No	☑ Yes
Example	Visual schedule, Braille	Reduce number of questions
Impact on Grade-level	None	May result in alternate grading

✨ Final Takeaway

◆ **Adaptations** help students **reach the same goals differently**
◆ **Modifications** help students **reach achievable goals meaningfully**
◆ Both ensure **inclusive and learner-friendly classrooms** 🏫

🧩 7. Multi-Sensory Teaching Approaches 🎡

💭 What Is Multi-Sensory Teaching?

Multi-sensory teaching is an approach where learning happens through **more than one sense** — typically involving **Visual (see), Auditory (hear), Kinesthetic (move), and Tactile (touch)** modalities.

https://www.specialeducationnotes.in

🎨 Imagine This: A Day in a Multi-Sensory Classroom

👩 *Ms. Kavita is teaching spellings to Class 2.*
She:

- 🗣 Says the word out loud (**auditory**)

- 👀 Writes it on the board in big, colorful letters (**visual**)

- 🤲 Gives students sand trays to trace letters (**tactile**)

- 🧍 Makes them form letters using body poses (**kinesthetic**)

👉 That's **multi-sensory teaching** — same lesson, *multiple inputs*.

🎯 Why It Works (Especially for CWSN)

💡 Benefit	🎯 Impact
Engages multiple parts of the brain	Better understanding & memory
Supports different learning styles	Visual, auditory, kinesthetic learners feel included
Helps children with LD, ADHD, Autism	Reduces cognitive load, increases focus
Boosts participation	Even shy or struggling learners feel confident

---

🧩 4 Pillars: The VAKT Model

Sense	Teaching Strategy	Example
Visual (V)	Show pictures, diagrams, colors	Charts, mind maps, flashcards
Auditory (A)	Say out loud, sing, use rhythm	Rhymes, reading aloud, chants

| Kinesthetic (K) | Use body movement or gestures | Role play, dance, jump to answer |
| Tactile (T) | Use touch-based activities | Clay modeling, sand tracing, puzzles |

🎨 *A child with dyslexia may struggle with reading—but when taught via songs, tracing, and flashcards, the same child can shine!*

📘 Multi-Sensory Techniques by Subject

🗃 Subject	💡 Multi-Sensory Idea
Math	Use real coins, counting beads, dance for numbers
English	Trace letters in sand, use phonics songs
Science	Perform experiments, model organs with clay
EVS/SST	Storytelling, role play historical events

🔍 Case Study: Rani & the Magic Letters

Rani, a student with dysgraphia, couldn't write well and was frustrated. Her teacher used **multi-sensory phonics**:

- Sky writing letters in air ✍
- Singing alphabet sounds 🎵
- Building letters using clay ⚪
- Listening to phonics stories 🎧
  ✅ Within months, Rani could recognize and spell 20 new words!

🎓 What the Research Says

According to Orton-Gillingham & Montessori methods, multi-sensory learning:

- Activates **neural pathways more deeply** 🧠

- Improves **attention and retention** in special learners

- Is especially effective for **dyslexia, ADHD, ASD & LD**

📜 Policies That Promote It

📄 Document	What It Says
NEP 2020	Promotes activity-based, flexible learning styles
NCF 2023	Recommends multi-sensory tools in early grades
RPwD Act 2016	Supports alternate and adapted teaching methods
Samagra Shiksha	Encourages inclusive and creative pedagogy

✅ Quick Check (Flash Quiz!)

1. Multi-sensory learning supports:
   A) Only visual learners
   B) Only gifted children
   C) All types of learners
   ✅ **Answer:** C

2. Which of these is **not** a tactile activity?
   A) Tracing in sand
   B) Listening to audio
   C) Playing with textures
   ✅ **Answer:** B

3. Which method is most suitable for a child with **dyslexia**?
    A) Lecture only
    B) Visual + auditory + tactile combo
    ✅ **Answer:** B

📋 Bonus: 5 Ready-to-Use Activities for Classrooms

1. **Word Hopscotch** – Jump on correct letters

2. **Touch & Match** – Match textures with objects

3. **Clap the Syllables** – Learn rhythm in words

4. **Color Code Notes** – For visual organization

5. **Sing Your Lesson** – Turn facts into a song 🎵

✨ Final Takeaway

✅ **Multi-sensory learning is NOT just a method, it's a mindset.**
✅ It values **diversity in learning** and gives **every child a chance to succeed.**
✅ Essential for children with **LD, ADHD, ASD, or any learning barriers.**

🧩 *8. Types of Disorders: Developmental, Personality & Abnormal Psychology* 🧠

🎯 OVERVIEW AT A GLANCE

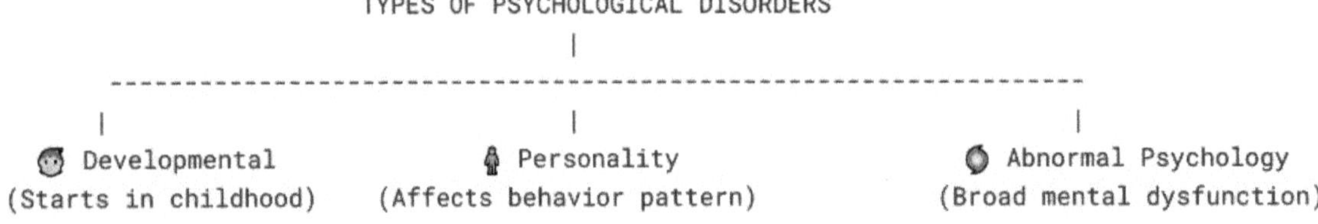

    https://www.specialeducationnotes.in

1 Developmental Disorders

Definition: Disorders that appear **during the developmental period** (childhood or early adolescence), affecting **cognitive, motor, social, or emotional growth**.

Key Types & Features:

Disorder	Main Features	Examples
Autism Spectrum Disorder (ASD)	Impaired social interaction, repetitive behavior	No eye contact, rigid routines
ADHD	Inattention, impulsivity, hyperactivity	Difficulty focusing, talks excessively
Learning Disabilities (LD)	Difficulty in reading, writing, math	Dyslexia, Dyscalculia
Intellectual Disability (ID)	Low IQ, poor adaptive behavior	Delayed milestones
Speech & Language Disorders	Trouble speaking/understanding	Stuttering, aphasia

Exam Fact:

ADHD is more common in **boys** than girls; often co-exists with learning problems.
PYQ-based Tip!

---

2 Personality Disorders

Definition: Long-term patterns of thinking, feeling, and behaving that deviate from social expectations and cause problems in **relationships, work, or daily life**.

3 Personality Disorder Clusters:

Cluster	Type	Traits
A (Odd/Eccentric)	Paranoid, Schizoid, Schizotypal	Suspicious, detached
B (Dramatic/Emotional)	Borderline, Narcissistic, Antisocial, Histrionic	Impulsive, emotional, manipulative

C (Anxious/Fearful) Avoidant, Dependent, Obsessive-Compulsive Clingy, perfectionist

✷ Famous Examples:

- **Borderline PD** – Fear of abandonment, emotional instability

- **Narcissistic PD** – Inflated self-image, need for admiration

- **Obsessive-Compulsive PD** – Extreme orderliness, rigidity (not same as OCD)

⬭ Mnemonic for Clusters:
A = Alone, **B** = Bold, **C** = Clingy

---

3 Abnormal Psychology

◉ *Definition:* The scientific study of unusual patterns of behavior, emotion, and thought — often relating to **mental illness** or **psychopathology**.

🌐 Core Areas:

Domain	Includes Disorders Like…
Mood Disorders	Depression, Bipolar Disorder
Anxiety Disorders	Phobia, Panic Disorder, GAD
Psychotic Disorders	Schizophrenia, Delusional Disorder
Somatic Disorders	Conversion Disorder, Illness Anxiety
Dissociative Disorders	Amnesia, Multiple Personality (DID)
Obsessive-Compulsive Related	OCD, Hoarding Disorder
Eating Disorders	Anorexia, Bulimia
Substance Use Disorders	Alcoholism, Drug dependence

🔍 Abnormal ≠ Bad

Not all abnormal behavior is **mental illness**. Culture, stress, and situation matter.

📚 KEY DIFFERENCES TABLE

Feature	Developmental	Personality	Abnormal
Onset	Childhood	Adolescence/early adulthood	Any time
Duration	Lifelong	Chronic	May be episodic or chronic
Focus	Development delays	Behavior patterns	Broad mental dysfunction
Treatment	Therapy + Support	Psychotherapy	Psychiatry + therapy

🧠 PYQs (Previous Year Questions)

1. **CTET 2021:** ADHD is a type of—
   A) Personality Disorder
   B) Developmental Disorder
   C) Psychotic Disorder
   D) Anxiety Disorder
   ✅ **Answer:** B

2. **DSSSB 2020:** Schizophrenia is best categorized under—
   A) Learning disability
   B) Mood disorder
   C) Psychotic disorder
   D) Personality disorder
   ✅ **Answer:** C

✍️ PRACTICE MCQs

1. Which disorder is associated with hallucinations and delusions?
   A) Depression
   B) OCD

C) Schizophrenia
D) ADHD
☑ **Answer:** C

2. A student has difficulty sitting still, frequently interrupts and is easily distracted. He may have:
   A) Autism
   B) OCD
   C) ADHD
   D) Bipolar Disorder
   ☑ **Answer:** C

3. Obsessive cleanliness, perfectionism, and need for control are features of:
   A) OCD
   B) OCPD
   C) GAD
   D) PTSD
   ☑ **Answer:** B

🎯 Important things -

- 👶 **Developmental Disorders** = Begin in childhood

- 🧍 **Personality Disorders** = Deep-rooted behavioral issues

- 🧠 **Abnormal Psychology** = The wider umbrella of mental health conditions

📌 *Understanding the types helps us adapt teaching, behavior management, and emotional support.*

🧩 9. Psychological Therapies: CBT, ABA & PBS 💭

🏫 Welcome to the Therapy Room!

Meet our three therapy stars:

🧩 Therapy	🧑‍💼 Full Form	⬤ Focus Area	👥 Commonly Used For
CBT	Cognitive Behavioral Therapy	Change negative thought-behavior cycle	Depression, anxiety, ADHD, Autism
ABA	Applied Behavior Analysis	Modify behavior using reinforcement	Autism Spectrum Disorder (ASD)
PBS	Positive Behavior Support	Promote positive behavior + reduce problem behaviors	Behavioral challenges in inclusive settings

⬤ 1. Cognitive Behavioral Therapy (CBT)

💡 *"Change the way you think to change the way you feel."*

🧩 Core Idea:

CBT helps people identify **negative thought patterns**, challenge them, and replace them with **rational, positive thoughts**.

▢ Example:

Ravi, a student with anxiety, thinks: *"Everyone will laugh at me if I answer."*
In CBT, he learns to reframe this as: *"Some may not agree, but I can still express my thoughts."*

💼 CBT Techniques:

Technique	Description
Cognitive Restructuring	Identifying and challenging irrational thoughts
Behavioral Experiments	Testing fears through real-life tasks
Thought Records	Journaling thoughts and analyzing patterns
Exposure Therapy	Gradual facing of feared situations

☁ CBT In Education:

- Helps children with **test anxiety, bullying issues, social fears**

- Encourages **self-reflection, problem-solving, emotional regulation**

  ☑ **CBT = Best for children who are verbal and can reflect on thoughts**

📊 CBT QUICK FACTS TABLE

Parameter	CBT
Time	Short-term (8–20 sessions)
Focus	Thoughts & behavior
Suitable for	Older children, teens, adults
Involves	Talking, worksheets, role play
Evidence-Based ?	☑ Highly researched

☁ 2. Applied Behavior Analysis (ABA)

💡 *"What gets rewarded, gets repeated."*

◎ Core Principle:

ABA uses **rewards and consequences** to teach desired behaviors and reduce unwanted ones.

💼 ABA Techniques:

Technique	What It Does
Positive Reinforcement	Give reward when desired behavior occurs
Prompting & Fading	Give hints, then gradually reduce them
Task Analysis	Break big tasks into small steps

Shaping   Reinforce closer versions of the target behavior

😊 Used Most Often For:

- Children with **Autism**

- **Non-verbal children**

- Functional skill building (e.g., brushing teeth, requesting help)

🍀 *Example:*
A child is taught to say "Water" by first reinforcing any attempt ("Wa…"), then full word ("Water"), using chocolates or praise.

💭 ABA = Highly structured, step-by-step, goal-driven.

📊 ABA QUICK FACTS TABLE

Parameter	ABA
Time	Long-term, daily
Focus	Behavior modification
Suitable for	Young children with ASD
Tools	Visuals, tokens, schedules
Evidence-Based ?	✅ Proven effective in Autism intervention

💭 3. Positive Behavior Support (PBS)

💡 *"Don't punish the behavior. Understand the reason behind it."*

🌱 Core Idea:

PBS focuses on **preventing problem behavior** by **understanding its cause** and promoting **positive alternatives**.

💼 PBS Involves:

Strategy	Explanation
Functional Behavior Assessment (FBA)	Analyze "Why is the child doing this?"
Antecedent Modifications	Change triggers (e.g., reduce noise)
Teaching Alternative Behaviors	Replace shouting with raising hand
Environmental Support	Visual schedules, sensory breaks

👩‍🏫 In the Classroom:

- Use **praise, tokens, peer modeling**

- Set clear rules, use visuals, give breaks

⚪ PBS is **preventive**, **respectful**, and supports inclusion for children with **ADHD, Autism, Behavioral Issues**

📖 *Case Study:*
Aman often throws books. PBS team discovers he throws books when confused. Solution? Add visuals + extra instruction time = ▣ ☑ calmer classroom!

📊 PBS QUICK FACTS TABLE

Parameter	PBS
Time	Ongoing
Focus	Understanding & prevention
Suitable for	Inclusive classrooms
Involves	Teachers + parents + child
Evidence-Based ?	☑ Especially for behavioral challenges

🔄 Compare the Three Therapies (Revision Booster Table)

Feature	CBT	ABA	PBS
Based on	Thoughts & beliefs	Operant Conditioning	Behavior + Environment
Ideal for	Anxiety, Depression	Autism, LD	ADHD, Behavioral Issues
Method	Talking & reflection	Reinforcement techniques	Understanding triggers
Approach	Individual	Structured 1:1	Collaborative with teachers/family
Age	Older kids & adults	Mostly young children	Any age

🎓 PYQs & MCQs

1. **CBT is based on the connection between:**
   A) Behavior and rewards
   B) Thoughts, feelings, and behavior
   ☑ **Answer:** B

2. **Which therapy is most suitable for autistic children using token systems?**
   A) CBT
   B) ABA
   ☑ **Answer:** B

3. **Positive Behavior Support focuses on:**
   A) Punishing bad behavior
   B) Identifying causes & teaching alternatives
   ☑ **Answer:** B

✨ Important things -

- 🎯 **CBT**: Think better → Feel better

- 🧩 **ABA**: Reinforce the right behavior

- 🦴 **PBS**: Understand & support, not punish

Each of these therapies helps make classrooms more inclusive, and students more independent and emotionally healthy. 🏛️

🧩 10. Occupational Psychology & Therapy 🪨

◆ Part 1: Occupational Psychology

— *"The Psychology of Work & Performance"*

💡 What is it?

Occupational Psychology is the study of **human behavior in workplaces**. It uses psychological principles to improve **productivity**, **job satisfaction**, **employee well-being**, and **organizational efficiency**.

📖 Also called *Industrial-Organizational Psychology*.

🔧 Core Functions

Area	What It Covers	Example
Recruitment & Selection	Psychometric testing, interviews	Aptitude tests for hiring teachers
Training & Development	Skills training, motivation programs	Workshops to improve classroom management
Performance Appraisal	Setting KPIs, feedback systems	Teacher performance review system
Workplace Mental Health	Stress management, burnout prevention	Support groups for school staff
Leadership & Teamwork	Team building, leadership styles	Principals using democratic leadership

☁ Key Concepts in Education

- **Motivation Theories** (Maslow, Herzberg)

- **Job Satisfaction** = Higher teacher retention

- **Work-Life Balance** = Reduced teacher burnout

◎ PYQ Snapshot (DSSSB 2022):

Q: Occupational psychology helps in—
A) Diagnosing mental illness
B) Enhancing workplace performance
C) Managing classroom behavior
D) Designing curriculum
☑ **Answer:** B

◆ Part 2: Occupational Therapy (OT)

— *"Helping People Participate in Life Fully"*

💡 What is it?

Occupational Therapy helps individuals with **physical, sensory, or cognitive challenges** gain independence in **daily life activities** (occupations) — like dressing, writing, or feeding.

> 🖼 In schools, it helps children with disabilities participate in classroom and play activities.

☺ Target Population

- **Children with Developmental Delays** (Autism, ADHD, Down Syndrome)

- **Physically Handicapped Children**

- **Learning Disabilities**

- **Sensory Processing Issues**

💼 OT Activities in School Settings

Area	OT Support
Fine Motor Skills	Pencil grasp, scissor use
Gross Motor Skills	Balance, posture during writing
Sensory Integration	Over/under response to sound, touch
Daily Living Skills	Buttoning shirt, using the toilet
Classroom Participation	Holding pencil, cutting paper, using rulers

---

👩‍🏫 Role of Occupational Therapist in School

Task	Example
Classroom modifications	Special seating, slant boards
Collaboration with teachers	Creating IEP goals
Sensory breaks planning	"Jumping jacks time" every 30 minutes
Monitoring progress	Tracking motor skill development

📊 Difference Table: Occupational Psychology vs. Occupational Therapy

Feature	Occupational Psychology	Occupational Therapy
Focus	Workplace behavior & performance	Daily life skills in people with disabilities
Work Setting	Corporate, educational leadership	Schools, hospitals, rehab centers

| Clients | Employees, managers, staff | Children, students, adults with disabilities |
| Goals | Improve job satisfaction & efficiency | Enable independence in everyday tasks |

🪨 Real-Life Classroom Application

Case Example:

A child with Cerebral Palsy struggles to hold a pencil.
◆ **OT** gives him a pencil grip + slanted board.
◆ **Occupational Psychologist** trains teachers to support inclusive practices and reduce staff stress.

📝 Practice MCQs

1. **Occupational Therapy mainly focuses on:**
   A) Career counseling
   B) Enhancing daily living activities
   C) Improving emotional intelligence
   D) Managing classroom discipline
   ☑ **Answer:** B

2. **An occupational therapist is helping a student with pencil grip. This addresses:**
   A) Cognitive delays
   B) Gross motor skills
   C) Fine motor skills
   D) Behavioral issues
   ☑ **Answer:** C

3. **Occupational Psychology is useful for:**
   A) Treating physical disabilities
   B) Improving teacher work performance
   C) Teaching social skills
   D) Conducting hearing tests
   ☑ **Answer:** B

◎ Important things –

| 💬 Psychology | = Better work behavior & productivity | | 🫳 Therapy | = Better everyday functioning & independence |

Both are **key pillars in inclusive education** – helping children, teachers, and systems perform at their best! 🧑‍🤝‍🧑

5 Assessment & Evaluation in Special Education

☁ *Types of Assessment in Special Education*

"Assessing differently-abled learners requires different lenses."

Assessment in Special Education is not about comparing one child to another — it is about **understanding individual progress**, **identifying needs**, and **guiding instruction** in a way that supports each learner's potential.

Here we explore the four most essential types of assessment used by special educators:

---

1 Formative Assessment

▉ *"Assessment for Learning"*

Formative assessment is a **continuous process** used during teaching to monitor learning progress and provide feedback. It helps educators adjust their instruction in real-time.

Feature	Description
Purpose	To track progress and inform instructional decisions
When it's used	During lessons or activities
Tools & Techniques	Observations, checklists, quizzes, portfolios, anecdotal records

| Significance for CWSN | Tracks micro-progress and helps modify IEP goals on the go |

| Example | A teacher observes a child's use of sign language during classroom routines |

Formative = Ongoing + Feedback-oriented

---

2 Summative Assessment

"Assessment of Learning"

Summative assessment is conducted **at the end of an instructional cycle** to evaluate the overall learning outcomes.

Feature	Description
Purpose	To measure achievement after instruction
When it's used	End of a unit, term, or IEP cycle
Tools & Techniques	Written tests, oral presentations, standardized exams, final projects
Significance for CWSN	Provides data to assess overall progress and revise long-term goals
Example	An end-of-term test measuring math skills in a child with dyscalculia

Summative = End-point evaluation

---

3 Diagnostic Assessment

"Assessment Before Learning"

This is a **pre-assessment** conducted before instruction begins. It identifies strengths, weaknesses, prior knowledge, and possible disabilities.

Feature	Description
Purpose	To detect learning gaps, disabilities, and readiness levels
When it's used	Prior to instruction or at the time of admission/IEP formulation
Tools & Techniques	Psychological assessments, screening tools, medical history, interviews
Significance for CWSN	Critical for IEP creation, disability identification, and placement decisions
Example	Diagnosing ADHD using behavioral checklists and clinical interviews

▪ *Diagnostic = Foundation for Individual Planning*

---

4 Dynamic Assessment

▪ *"Assessment With Support"*

This assessment evaluates a student's ability to learn **when guided**, based on **Vygotsky's Zone of Proximal Development (ZPD)**.

Feature	Description
Purpose	To assess learning potential with mediated help
When it's used	During interactive learning sessions
Tools & Techniques	Prompting, scaffolding tasks, mediated questioning
Significance for CWSN	Uncovers hidden abilities in children with cognitive or communication delays
Example	A speech therapist modeling a sentence structure, then observing repetition attempts

▪ *Dynamic = Focus on potential, not just current performance*

---

https://www.specialeducationnotes.in

🔄 Flowchart: When & Why to Use Each Type

```
Start Teaching
      ↓
   Do I know the child's needs?
          → No → Diagnostic Assessment
          → Yes ↓

Is learning happening as expected?
          → Not sure → Formative Assessment
          → Yes ↓

Is this the end of a topic/unit?
          → Yes → Summative Assessment
          → No ↓

Can the child improve with support?
          → Try → Dynamic Assessment
```

📊 Quick Comparison Table

Type of Assessment	When It's Used	Main Purpose	Example in Special Education
Formative	During learning	Guide & adjust teaching	Teacher modifies activities based on behavior
Summative	After learning	Evaluate outcomes	Term-end report on progress in functional skills
Diagnostic	Before learning	Identify needs/gaps	Dyslexia screening before literacy training
Dynamic	With support	Discover learning potential	Task-based guidance for ASD child in communication

✅ MCQs for Practice

1. Which type of assessment is most helpful in setting IEP goals for a new student?
a) Formative
b) Summative
c) Diagnostic
d) Dynamic
👉 **Answer: c) Diagnostic**

2. Vygotsky's Zone of Proximal Development is associated with:
a) Summative Assessment
b) Diagnostic Assessment
c) Formative Assessment
d) Dynamic Assessment
👉 **Answer: d) Dynamic Assessment**

3. Which assessment helps identify whether a student needs immediate instructional change?
a) Summative
b) Formative
c) Diagnostic
d) None of the above
👉 **Answer: b) Formative**

💼 *Tools & Techniques Used in Special Education*

"Teaching is not one-size-fits-all — especially when every learner is unique!"

Educators in Special Education use a variety of **tools (✂️)** and **techniques (📋)** to support the learning, communication, and behavioral needs of children with special needs (CWSN). These approaches ensure **inclusive, accessible, and personalized education** for all.

✊ 1. Assistive Technology Tools

"Devices that empower independence!"

✂️ Tool	🔍 Purpose	🙂 Example
Screen Readers	Helps students with visual impairments	JAWS, NVDA 📢

Speech-to-Text Software	Supports children with writing issues	Dragon NaturallySpeaking
AAC Devices	Helps in communication	PECS, Proloquo2Go
Braille Tools	Reading/writing for the blind	Perkins Brailler, Braille slate
Hearing Aids/FM Systems	Improves hearing & classroom listening	Phonak Roger Mic

These tools make learning more accessible, reduce barriers, and boost confidence.

---

2. Instructional Techniques

"Teach smart. Teach differently."

Technique	Description	Useful For...
Multi-sensory Teaching	Combines visual, auditory, kinesthetic input	Dyslexia, ADHD
Task Analysis	Breaks tasks into smaller steps	Autism, ID
Scaffolding	Gradual support, slowly reduced	Slow learners, LD
Errorless Learning	Prevents mistakes while learning	Autism, ID
Reinforcement	Rewards positive behavior	ADHD, ED

Smart teaching strategies = better learning outcomes!

---

3. Behavioral Techniques

"Behavior is communication — learn to shape it."

🎯 Technique	🧩 Purpose/Use	🔍 Example
Positive Reinforcement	Rewards good behavior	Stickers after task completion 🏆
Token Economy	Earn tokens, exchange for reward	5 stars = Extra playtime ⭐ 🎮
Time-Out	Remove from environment temporarily	Cool-down corner 🧩⏳
Modeling	Demonstrate the correct behavior	Showing how to greet 👋
Social Stories	Teach social skills through stories	"How to ask for help?" 📖👥🙂

💬 *Effective for managing emotions, routines, and social behaviors.*

👩‍🏫 4. Communication Tools

"Every child deserves a voice."

📋 Tool	🎯 Function	🧒 Used by...
PECS (Picture Exchange)	Non-verbal communication	Children with Autism 🖼️ ➡️ 💬
Sign Language	Gesture-based language	Deaf/Hard of Hearing 👋🤟
Voice Output Devices	Converts input to spoken words	Speech-impaired students 🔊👩‍🏫
Communication Boards	Board with symbols for interaction	Children with multiple disabilities 🙂🖼️

🔊 *Helps build connection, reduce frustration, and support classroom inclusion.*

🧩 5. Educational Materials & Modifications

"Small changes, big differences!"

🔲 Material/Modification	⊚ Purpose	📝 Example
Large Print Books	Aid for low vision	Big font textbooks 📖🔍
Color-Coded Notes	Organize & improve focus	Red = Math, Blue = Science ⬛⚫
Visual Schedules	Routine structure	Picture calendar 📅📷
Graphic Organizers	Organize thoughts	Concept maps, Venn diagrams 💬🗺️
Preferential Seating	Improve attention	Seat near teacher or window 🚪🧍

☐ *These tools promote clarity, predictability, and better engagement.*

🕐 Quick Recap: Tools vs Techniques

```
Tools = Physical Aids & Devices
   ↳ e.g., Braille, AAC devices, Hearing aids

Techniques = Teaching/Behavior Strategies
   ↳ e.g., Scaffolding, Task Analysis, Reinforcement
```

📝 Practice MCQs

1. Which of the following is a communication tool for non-verbal children?
a) Graphic Organizer
b) PECS
c) Time-out
d) FM System
☞ **Answer:** b) PECS

2. Breaking down a task into steps is called:
a) Modeling
b) Errorless Learning
c) Task Analysis

d) Token Economy
👉 **Answer:** c) Task Analysis

3. Which method uses rewards to improve behavior?
a) Task Analysis
b) Positive Reinforcement
c) Braille Tool
d) Visual Schedule
👉 **Answer:** b) Positive Reinforcement

4. What kind of tool is "Dragon NaturallySpeaking"?
a) Communication Board
b) Text-to-Speech Software
c) Speech-to-Text Software
d) Social Story Generator
👉 **Answer:** c) Speech-to-Text Software

🖊️ *Standardized vs Non-Standardized Assessments*

"Assessment is not just about marks, it's about understanding the learner!"

In Special Education, selecting the **right type of assessment** is crucial. Educators often use both **Standardized** and **Non-Standardized** tools depending on the purpose — whether it's for **diagnosis**, **instructional planning**, or **progress tracking**.

✏️ 1. Standardized Assessments

📎 *"One size fits most"*

✅ Definition:

Assessments that are **administered and scored in a consistent, uniform manner**. These are developed by experts, tested on large populations, and follow fixed guidelines.

💭 Purpose:

To **compare** an individual's performance with a **norm group** (average performance of same-age peers).

📌 Features:

- Fixed content & scoring

- High reliability & validity

- Norm-referenced

- Administered under strict conditions

- Often used for **diagnosis or eligibility**

✂️ Examples:

Test	Use Area
Wechsler Intelligence Scale (WISC)	Measures IQ & cognitive skills
Vineland Adaptive Behavior Scales	Adaptive functioning (for ID, ASD)
Stanford-Binet Test	General intelligence assessment
Woodcock-Johnson Tests	Academic achievement

📊 *These are used for formal decisions – e.g., identifying Intellectual Disability or LD.*

🪨 2. Non-Standardized Assessments

☐ *"Flexible, personalized, and informal"*

☑️ Definition:

Assessments that **do not follow uniform procedures**. These are more flexible and often customized to individual student needs.

🧠 Purpose:

To understand a student's **learning style, interests, progress**, and **daily classroom performance**.

     https://www.specialeducationnotes.in

📌 Features:

- No fixed format or scoring

- Teacher-designed

- Contextual & ongoing

- Helps in **instructional planning**

- Not used for formal diagnosis

🛠️ Examples:

Tool	Use Area
Anecdotal Records	Observing behaviors or habits
Checklist / Rating Scales	Skill tracking
Work Sample Analysis	Evaluating student tasks
Teacher-Made Tests	Lesson-specific assessment
Portfolio Assessment	Collecting student work over time

🧩 *Helps in daily feedback, IEP development, and individualized strategies.*

🆚 Standardized vs Non-Standardized: Comparison Table

Criteria	🖊️ Standardized Assessment	✏️ Non-Standardized Assessment
Structure	Fixed & Formal	Flexible & Informal
Purpose	Diagnostic / Comparative	Instructional / Progress Monitoring
Scoring	Pre-determined, objective	Varies, subjective or descriptive
Examples	IQ tests, Achievement tests	Observations, Teacher-made tests
Used For	Eligibility, Classification	Classroom planning, Daily monitoring

https://www.specialeducationnotes.in

| **Evaluator** | Psychologists / Trained Assessors | Teachers / Special Educators |

💭 Quick Memory Tip:

**"Standardized = Standard rules, Standard results.
Non-Standardized = No rules, Personalized results."** 😄

📝 Practice MCQs

1. Which of the following is an example of a standardized test?
a) Portfolio Assessment
b) Teacher-made Quiz
c) WISC-IV
d) Anecdotal Record
👉 **Answer:** c) WISC-IV

2. Non-standardized assessment is most useful for:
a) Eligibility for Special Education
b) Comparing with national norms
c) Daily classroom planning
d) Diagnosing Autism
👉 **Answer:** c) Daily classroom planning

3. Which assessment is likely to involve strict administration rules?
a) Checklist
b) Anecdotal Note
c) Standardized IQ Test
d) Portfolio
👉 **Answer:** c) Standardized IQ Test

4. Teacher-made tests are an example of:
a) Norm-referenced tools
b) Standardized assessments
c) Non-standardized assessments
d) Screening tests
👉 **Answer:** c) Non-standardized assessments

🪨 *Intelligence Tests: Wechsler Intelligence Scale for Children (WISC)*

"Every child is smart, but we need the right tools to understand how they're smart." 🧩

📌 What is the WISC?

The **Wechsler Intelligence Scale for Children (WISC)** is a **standardized intelligence test** developed by **David Wechsler** to measure the **intellectual ability** of children aged **6 to 16 years**. 🪨🖊

> 🖊 It is widely used in **Special Education** to assess children's cognitive profiles, strengths, and support needs.

🎯 Purpose of WISC

- ✅ To determine **IQ Score** (Intelligence Quotient)
- ✅ Identify **Learning Disabilities (LD)** or **Intellectual Disability (ID)**
- ✅ Support **IEP planning**
- ✅ Diagnose **developmental delays, ADHD, Autism Spectrum Disorders**

🏛 Structure of WISC-V (Latest Version)

WISC-V consists of **10 core subtests** across **5 primary index scores:**

🧩 Index	📖 What it Measures	🔍 Example Subtests
1. Verbal Comprehension (VCI)	Vocabulary, verbal reasoning	Similarities, Vocabulary 📚
2. Visual Spatial (VSI)	Visual & spatial problem solving	Block Design, Visual Puzzles 📦🧩
3. Fluid Reasoning (FRI)	Abstract thinking, logic	Matrix Reasoning, Figure Weights 🪨⚖

| 4. Working Memory (WMI) | Short-term memory, attention | Digit Span, Picture Span |
| 5. Processing Speed (PSI) | Speed & accuracy of simple tasks | Coding, Symbol Search |

📊 IQ Score Interpretation

💡 IQ Score Range	📌 Interpretation
130 and above	Very Superior
120 – 129	Superior
110 – 119	High Average
90 – 109	Average
80 – 89	Low Average
70 – 79	Borderline
Below 70	Extremely Low (ID suspected)

🌸 Importance in Special Education

🔑 Use	🖊 Explanation
Diagnosis	Helps identify LD, ADHD, or ID
IEP Planning	Targets strengths & weaknesses
Giftedness/Remediation	Selects students for special programs
Progress Tracking	Used in pre/post evaluations

✅ Advantages of WISC

- Scientifically **reliable & valid**

- Gives a **detailed cognitive profile**

- Widely accepted in schools

- Useful for both **diagnosis** and **intervention planning**

⚠ Limitations of WISC

- Needs trained psychologist

- Time-consuming (1–1.5 hrs)

- May show cultural/language bias

- Doesn't measure creativity or emotional intelligence

📝 MCQs + Previous Year Questions (PYQs)

◎ Practice MCQs

1. WISC is suitable for which age group?
a) 3 to 7 years
b) 6 to 16 years ✓
c) 10 to 20 years
d) 2 to 12 years
☞ **Answer:** b) 6 to 16 years

2. The 'Processing Speed Index' in WISC measures:
a) Creativity
b) Memory
c) Speed of task completion ✓
d) Language ability
☞ **Answer:** c) Speed of task completion

Q1. *Which of the following is a standardized test used for measuring intelligence in children?*
(DSSSB 2021)
a) Stanford Achievement Test
b) Wechsler Intelligence Scale for Children ☑
c) CARS
d) Bender Gestalt Test
👉 **Answer:** b) Wechsler Intelligence Scale for Children

Q2. *A 9-year-old child is unable to concentrate and shows signs of attention issues. Which subtest of WISC would be most relevant?*
(KVS 2019)
a) Verbal Comprehension
b) Working Memory ☑
c) Visual Spatial
d) Fluid Reasoning
👉 **Answer:** b) Working Memory

Q3. *Full-Scale IQ in WISC-V is obtained by combining scores from:*
(CTET 2020)
a) Only verbal subtests
b) Non-verbal tasks
c) All 5 index scores ☑
d) Adaptive behavior rating scales
👉 **Answer:** c) All 5 index scores

Q4. *A score below 70 on WISC suggests:*
(DSSSB 2022)
a) Giftedness
b) Normal intelligence
c) Intellectual Disability ☑
d) Learning disability
👉 **Answer:** c) Intellectual Disability

Memory Trick:

WISC = Wechsler's Intelligence Scale for Children
🧒 Age: **6 to 16 years**
5 Indexes → IQ score → Special Education planning 🧩 ☑

🪨 *Adaptive Behavior Scale: Vineland Adaptive Behavior Scale (VABS)*

*"It's not just what a child knows… it's what a child **can do in daily life** that matters!"* 🧩

📌 What is Adaptive Behavior?

Adaptive Behavior refers to the ability of a person to meet **everyday demands** of their environment and function independently in **real-life situations**.

> ☑ It includes skills like **communication**, **self-care**, **social interaction**, **problem-solving**, and more.

📋 What is VABS?

The **Vineland Adaptive Behavior Scale (VABS)** is a **standardized tool** used to **measure adaptive behavior** in individuals from **birth to 90 years**.

📍 **Developed by:** Edgar A. Doll (original), later revised by Sparrow, Cicchetti & Balla
📍 **Latest version:** Vineland-3
📍 **Used for:** Diagnosing **Intellectual Disability**, **Autism**, **Developmental Delay**, **ADHD**, etc.

🧩 Domains of Vineland Adaptive Behavior Scale

📚 Domain	📝 Description
1. Communication 🗣	Understanding & expressing through spoken/written language

2. Daily Living Skills 🖐️   Self-care, dressing, eating, hygiene, household tasks

3. Socialization 💟   Interpersonal skills, relationships, play, empathy, following rules

4. Motor Skills 🏃   Fine & gross motor skills like running, holding objects (mostly in young children)

5. Maladaptive Behavior 🚫   (Optional) Behaviors that interfere with social/learning development

---

🏗️ Structure of VABS

🛠️ Feature	📋 Details
Format	Semi-structured interview / questionnaire
Respondents	Parents, teachers, caregivers 👨‍👩‍👧
Scoring	Adaptive scores for each domain (standardized)
Age Range	Birth to 90 years 👶
Time Required	20–60 minutes 🕐

🎯 Use of VABS in Special Education

🎯 Purpose	📝 Why it's important
◆ **Diagnosing Intellectual Disability (ID)**	Required for confirming adaptive behavior deficits
◆ **Autism Spectrum Disorders (ASD)**	Assesses social skills and daily living challenges
◆ **IEP Planning**	Helps personalize learning goals based on strengths/needs
◆ **Tracking Development**	Monitors progress in adaptive skills over time

✅ Advantages of VABS

✔ Covers real-life, **functional abilities**
✔ Applicable across **wide age range**
✔ Can be administered **indirectly** via parents/caregivers
✔ Highly useful for **eligibility determination** in Special Ed

⚠ Limitations

🚫 Relies on **subjective responses** of caregivers
🚫 Needs trained interviewer for accurate data
🚫 May not reflect **cultural/contextual** variations

📝 MCQs + Previous Year Questions (PYQs)

🔍 Practice MCQs

1. Vineland Adaptive Behavior Scale assesses:
a) Academic achievement
b) Intelligence
c) Adaptive functioning ✅
d) Emotional behavior
👉 **Answer:** c) Adaptive functioning

2. Which of the following is *not* a domain in VABS?
a) Communication
b) Motor Skills
c) Reasoning Ability ✅
d) Socialization
👉 **Answer:** c) Reasoning Ability

3. VABS is most useful in diagnosing:
a) Learning Disabilities
b) Intellectual Disability ✅
c) Visual Impairment

d) Hearing Loss

👉 **Answer:** b) Intellectual Disability

📖 PYQs (DSSSB / KVS / CTET)

Q1. *Which test is widely used to assess adaptive functioning in children?*
(DSSSB 2021)
a) Stanford Binet
b) CARS
c) WISC
d) Vineland Adaptive Behavior Scale ☑

👉 **Answer:** d) Vineland Adaptive Behavior Scale

Q2. *For diagnosing Intellectual Disability, which two areas must be assessed?*
(KVS 2019)
a) IQ and creativity
b) IQ and academic scores
c) IQ and adaptive behavior ☑
d) Social behavior and interests

👉 **Answer:** c) IQ and adaptive behavior

Q3. *VABS is suitable for which age range?*
(CTET 2020)
a) 3 to 18 years
b) 0 to 6 years
c) Birth to 90 years ☑
d) 2 to 10 years

👉 **Answer:** c) Birth to 90 years

💡 Quick Memory Tip:

Vineland = **V**ital **A**ctivities of daily life
Measures how well a child lives, plays, communicates, and behaves ☑

🪨 *Functional Behavior Assessment (FBA) & Behavioral Interventions*

"Behind every behavior, there's a reason — let's find it and fix it!" 🔍 ✂️

🔍 What is Functional Behavior Assessment (FBA)?

FBA is a **systematic process** used by special educators to understand **why a student shows challenging behavior**. Instead of focusing only on *what* the behavior is, it focuses on *why* it happens. This helps teachers and psychologists create strategies that reduce the behavior by addressing its **true cause**.

For example, if a child keeps throwing books in class, FBA helps us figure out **whether they're seeking attention, avoiding a task, feeling overwhelmed, or needing sensory input**. Once we know the *why*, we can create the *how* to solve it!

🧩 Key Steps in FBA (Explained Simply)

1. **Identifying the Problem Behavior** 🔺
   The behavior must be **clearly defined**. Instead of saying "He's being naughty," say "He hits his classmates during group activities."

2. **Collecting Data** 📋
   Teachers observe the child, interview caregivers, and sometimes use tools like **ABC charts** (Antecedent–Behavior–Consequence) to track what's happening before, during, and after the behavior.

3. **Analyzing the Data** 🔘
   Once data is collected, the educator looks for **patterns**. Does the child misbehave during a specific subject? Around a certain teacher? After recess?

4. **Finding the Function of Behavior** 🎯
   Behaviors usually serve one of these purposes:

   - To escape a situation (like a hard task) 🚪

   - To gain attention (from peers or adults) 👀

   https://www.specialeducationnotes.in

- To get something (a toy, food, break, etc.) 🎁

- To fulfill a sensory need (like rocking or hand-flapping) 🎧

5. **Planning an Intervention** ⚒️
   Strategies are created to **replace the negative behavior with a positive one**. For example, if a child hits to avoid work, teach them to request a break instead.

6. **Monitoring Progress** 🔄
   Regular checks are done to see if the intervention is working. If not, it is adjusted.

🌀 Understanding the "Function" of Behavior (With Examples)

Let's take a few examples to make this crystal clear:

- **Escape**: A student throws tantrums during math class. FBA might reveal they do this to avoid the difficult subject.

- **Attention**: A student frequently calls out in class. Observation shows they do it when they're not being noticed.

- **Access**: A child screams until given a toy. The behavior is to gain something they want.

- **Sensory**: A child rocks back and forth for long periods. They might be self-soothing or enjoying the motion.

Once we **know the function**, we can teach the child a **better way** to get the same need met — like asking for help or using a break card.

⚒️ Behavioral Interventions Based on FBA

The **intervention** must match the function of behavior. There is **no one-size-fits-all** solution. For example:

- If the child acts out to avoid tasks, give **shorter tasks, frequent breaks**, or **visual schedules**.

- For attention-seeking behavior, ignore negative actions and give **praise for positive behavior**.

- If the behavior is sensory, provide **safe sensory tools** like fidget toys or a calming space.

- Teach **replacement behaviors** — like raising a hand to speak instead of shouting.

These are called **Positive Behavior Support Strategies**, and they aim to **change behavior by teaching, not punishing**.

💼 Tools Used in FBA

While FBA relies heavily on **observation and interviews**, educators may also use tools like:

- **Behavior checklists**

- **Rating scales**

- **ABC data sheets**

- **Video analysis** (if allowed)

- **Parent/teacher input forms**

The goal is to get a **complete picture** of the child's behavior across settings.

📙 Real Exam Questions (PYQs & MCQs Style)

📝 MCQs for Practice

1. What is the primary purpose of Functional Behavior Assessment?
a) To punish misbehavior
b) To diagnose autism
c) To understand why a behavior occurs ✅
d) To test academic skills

👉 **Answer:** c) To understand why a behavior occurs

---

2. In FBA, "ABC" stands for:
a) Action – Behavior – Consequence
b) Antecedent – Behavior – Consequence ☑
c) Attention – Behavior – Control
d) Attitude – Belief – Confidence

👉 **Answer:** b) Antecedent – Behavior – Consequence

📖 PYQs

Q1. *FBA is an important component of:*
(KVS 2021)
a) Academic evaluation
b) IQ assessment
c) Positive Behavior Support ☑
d) Medical diagnosis

Q2. *Which is the first step in conducting FBA?*
(DSSSB 2022)
a) Creating a behavior chart
b) Interviewing parents
c) Identifying the target behavior ☑
d) Giving rewards

💡 Memory Trick

👉 FBA = **Find Behavior's Aim** 🎯
👉 ABC = **A**ntecedent → **B**ehavior → **C**onsequence

🧬 *Assessment of Different Disabilities (All 21 as per RPwD Act, 2016)*

"Different needs, different assessments — but one goal: Inclusion!" 💜

The **Rights of Persons with Disabilities (RPwD) Act, 2016** recognizes **21 types of disabilities**, each requiring a **specialized method of assessment**. Educators, psychologists, and therapists work together to understand the child's abilities, limitations, and support needs. Let's look at how these diverse conditions are assessed in the field of **special education**. 💬📝

🧠 1. Intellectual Disability (ID)

- **IQ Tests** like WISC or Stanford-Binet

- **Vineland Adaptive Behavior Scale (VABS)** to assess life skills

- **Developmental history + school performance review**

🧩 2. Autism Spectrum Disorder (ASD)

- Tools like **CARS**, **ADOS**, and **M-CHAT**

- Focus on **communication, social interaction, and repetitive behaviors**

- **Parent interview + direct observation** 🐾

⚡ 3. Specific Learning Disabilities (SLD)

Includes dyslexia, dyscalculia, dysgraphia, etc.

- **NIMHANS SLD Battery, DST-J, Woodcock-Johnson Tests**

- Performance in **reading, writing, math**

- Need to observe the **gap between ability and achievement**

🌀 4. Attention Deficit Hyperactivity Disorder (ADHD)

- **Conners Rating Scale, CBRS**, behavioral checklists

- Observation of **inattention, impulsivity, and hyperactivity** across settings

- **Rule out** other causes like anxiety or trauma

---

5. Hearing Impairment

- **Audiometry & Tympanometry** to test hearing level

- **Speech-language evaluation**

- **Functional hearing** in classrooms + use of hearing aids

---

6. Visual Impairment

- **Visual acuity test**, **field test**, and **color vision testing**

- **Functional Vision Assessment**: how the child uses sight in daily activities

- Need for **Braille** or **assistive devices**

---

7. Locomotor Disability

Affects movement of limbs, spine, or posture.

- **Physiotherapy evaluation**, strength and range of motion tests

- **Mobility aids** required? Wheelchair? Crutches?

- Educational barrier analysis (e.g., accessibility of classrooms)

---

8. Cerebral Palsy

A neurodevelopmental condition affecting **movement, balance & coordination**.

- **Gross Motor Function Classification System (GMFCS)**

- **Occupational Therapy assessment**

- Cognitive and speech-language checkups often included

💬 9. Speech and Language Disability

- **Receptive and expressive language tests**

- **Articulation assessment**

- Tools: **Reynell Developmental Language Scales, CCC-2, SLDT** 🗣️

🍬 10. Thalassemia & 🧬 11. Hemophilia

These are **blood disorders**.

- Require **medical reports, clinical evaluations**

- Assessment in school includes understanding **fatigue, absenteeism, need for medication, and emergency protocols**

🤍 12. Sickle Cell Disease

- Similar to thalassemia in educational impact

- Assess how **pain episodes, anemia, or fatigue** affect attendance, performance

---

⚪ 13. Multiple Disabilities (Including Deafblindness)

Combination of two or more impairments

- Requires **multi-domain assessments**

- Focus on **communication, mobility, self-help, cognition**

- **Functional needs** prioritized over labels

🧍 14. Dwarfism

- **Medical evaluation** for type & cause

- Focus on **social and emotional development**

- Check for **classroom seating, board visibility, toilet access** etc.

---

15. Muscular Dystrophy

A progressive condition affecting **muscle strength**

- **Physiotherapy assessment**, **fatigue level**, mobility testing

- Academic impact comes from **physical limitations** and **frequent medical care**

---

16. Acid Attack Victims

- **Physical + psychological evaluation**

- Need to assess **vision, mobility, communication**, and emotional trauma

- Social inclusion and **confidence-building** are major goals

---

⚡ 17. Parkinson's Disease

Rare in children, but in young adults it can affect **movement, speech, and mood**

- **Neurological examination, motor tests, cognitive screening**

💬 18. Chronic Neurological Conditions (e.g., Epilepsy)

- **Seizure history**, medication effects
- **Cognitive and psychosocial assessment**
- Monitor for **learning gaps** due to absenteeism

〰 19. Mental Illness (e.g., Depression, Bipolar)

- Assessed using **psychiatric tools** (e.g., DSM-5 criteria, CBCL, Beck's Scale)
- Observation of **emotional regulation, attention span, peer interaction**
- Classroom-based support planning

🖋 20. Multiple Sclerosis

(Autoimmune disorder affecting the brain & spinal cord)

- Rare in children, but if present: assess **fatigue, motor control, concentration**, and academic consistency

---

🔘 21. Learning Disabilities (Comprehensive Term)

Covers **developmental dyslexia, dysgraphia, dyscalculia** etc.
(Already explained above in point 3 but recognized separately under RPwD Act.)

☑ Summary Table (Just for Quick Recall):

Category	Examples	Assessment Tools Used
Cognitive/Developmental	ID, ASD, SLD, ADHD	WISC, CARS, NIMHANS SLD, Connors
Sensory	HI, VI, Deafblindness	Audiometry, Vision Test, FVA
Physical/Neuromotor	CP, Locomotor, Dwarfism, MD	GMFCS, PT Eval, Functional Mobility
Blood/Chronic Disorders	Thalassemia, Hemophilia, Sickle	Medical Reports, Fatigue/Functionality Check
Psychological/Neurological	Mental Illness, MS, Parkinson's	Psychiatric tools, Emotional/Social Screening
Multiple Disabilities	Mix of two or more conditions	Combined multidisciplinary assessment

---

📖 PYQ Practice (Previous Year Question Style)

1. *Which tool is used to assess children with learning disability in Indian schools?*
a) ADOS
b) NIMHANS SLD Battery ☑
c) BKT
d) VABS
👉 **Answer:** b) NIMHANS SLD Battery

2. *What is the full form of VABS used in assessment?*
a) Visual Ability Behavior Scale
b) Vineland Adaptive Behavior Scale ☑
c) Visual Attention Behavior Scale
d) Verbal Assessment Behavior Schedule
👉 **Answer:** b) Vineland Adaptive Behavior Scale

🎯 Final Note for Exams:

📌 Don't try to **mug up all 21** — instead:

- Know the **categories**

- Learn **most tested disabilities** in depth (ID, ASD, SLD, HI, VI, CP, ADHD)

- Be ready to **identify tools used in each**

- Use **smart acronyms** and grouping for memory

6 Assistive Technology & Support Services

Assistive Technology (AT) and Support Services help **children with disabilities** access education, communication, and daily living more effectively. These tools and services break barriers and **empower learners** to reach their full potential 💪📋

☁ Key Definitions

Term	Meaning
Assistive Technology (AT)	Any **device, software, or equipment** that helps a person with a disability perform daily tasks.
Support Services	Additional services like **therapy, counseling, and training** provided to students, teachers, and families to enhance learning outcomes.

✨ Types of Assistive Technology (With Examples)

Type	Description	Examples
👤 Communication Aids	Help in speaking or understanding language	Picture boards, speech-generating devices
👓 Visual Aids	Support students with visual impairment	Braille readers, screen readers, magnifiers
👂 Hearing Aids	Assist those with hearing loss	FM systems, hearing aids, captioning tools
✋ Mobility Aids	Improve physical movement	Wheelchairs, walkers, modified desks
🎹 Learning Aids	Help in reading, writing & math	Audiobooks, text-to-speech, talking calculators

🖼️ Diagram: Assistive Technology in Action

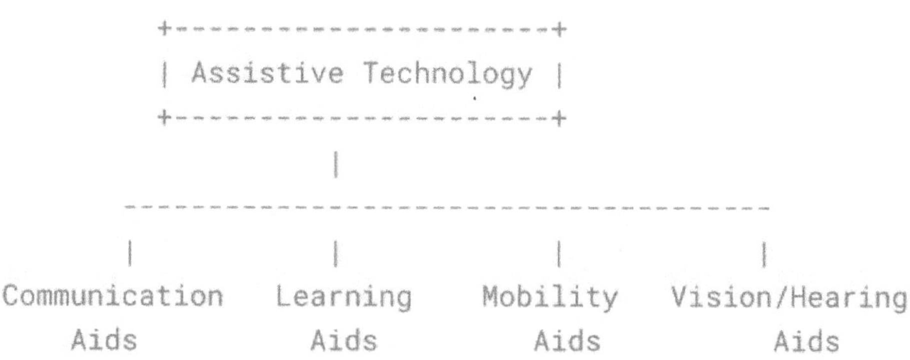

🎓 Support Services in Special Education

These services **complement AT** and are often offered by specialists:

Service	Role
👤 Occupational Therapy	Develops fine motor skills (e.g., using pencil grips)

🧑🏫 Special Educator	Designs Individualized Education Plans (IEPs)
👤 Counseling	Supports emotional and behavioral needs
🧑💻 AT Specialist	Trains students & teachers on using devices
🏠 Family Training	Helps families understand & use AT at home

🌟 *Importance of Assistive Technology in Special Education*

🎯 Introduction

Assistive Technology (AT) refers to **tools, devices, or systems** that help children with disabilities to **access education, communicate, and perform daily tasks** independently. 💬📱
It can range from **simple tools** (like pencil grips ✏️) to **high-tech gadgets** (like speech-generating devices 🧑‍💻💻).

💬 Why Is Assistive Technology Important in Special Education?

🔑 Reason	📖 Explanation
◆ **Access to Curriculum**	Helps children with disabilities to **participate fully** in classroom learning.
◆ **Enhanced Communication**	Devices like AAC boards allow **non-verbal students to express themselves**.
◆ **Boosts Independence**	Promotes self-reliance in tasks like reading, writing, mobility, etc.
◆ **Improves Self-Esteem**	Children feel more confident when they can perform tasks independently.
◆ **Promotes Inclusion**	Enables children to learn alongside their peers in **mainstream classrooms**.

<table>
<tr><td>◆ Supports Different Learning Styles</td><td>AT can be customized for visual, auditory, or kinesthetic learners.</td></tr>
</table>

✳️ Visual Mind Map: Importance of Assistive Technology

💡 Examples of Assistive Technology Tools

Type	Examples
Low-Tech	Pencil grips, Braille books, visual schedules
Mid-Tech	Audio books, talking calculators, magnifiers
High-Tech	Speech-to-text software, screen readers, electronic AAC devices

---

🎓 Real Impact in the Classroom

- A child with **dyslexia** can use **text-to-speech software** to read books aloud. 📖🎧

- A student with **hearing impairment** may benefit from **FM systems** for clear audio. 🎧

- A child with **limited mobility** can write using **voice recognition** instead of typing. ✏️

1. KVS 2018

Q: Which of the following is an example of high-tech assistive technology?
A. Braille Slate
B. FM Hearing System
C. Visual Schedule
D. Picture Exchange Cards
☑ **Correct Answer: B**

❓Practice MCQs

1. Assistive Technology helps students with disabilities to:
A. Rely on others
B. Learn passively
C. Become more independent
D. Avoid school
☑ **Correct Answer: C**

2. Which of the following is NOT an assistive technology device?
A. Braille Books
B. Textbooks
C. Voice Recognition Software
D. Audio Books
☑ **Correct Answer: B**

🔍 Quick Revision Box

🔘 Key Point	📄 Summary
What is AT?	Tools that aid learning for children with disabilities
Key Benefits	Access, communication, independence, inclusion
Types	Low, Mid, High-tech
Example Devices	Braille books, FM system, AAC devices

   https://www.specialeducationnotes.in

🚀 Types of Assistive Technology Devices in Special Education

(Low-Tech, Mid-Tech & High-Tech Devices)

🌀 Why Classify AT Devices?

Because not all children need fancy gadgets 💻— some just need **simple, effective tools**. Assistive Technology is classified based on:

- 💡 **Complexity** (simple → advanced)

- ⚙️ **Power needs**

- 💰 **Cost**

- 🎓 **Training required**

🎯 1. Low-Tech Assistive Devices – *Simple but Smart!* 💼

These are **non-electronic, easy-to-use, and inexpensive tools** that support children in learning, writing, organizing, and communicating.

📝 Key Features:

- No electricity or battery 🔋

- Low maintenance

- Easy for both teachers & students to handle

- Immediate usability in classrooms 💼

✅ **Popular Examples:**

📌 Tool	💬 Use Case
✏️ Pencil Grips	Helps with fine motor skills (e.g., in CP, LD)
📕 Braille Books	Reading material for blind students
🖼️ Picture Cards/PECS	Communication aid for children with autism
📇 Visual Schedules	Daily routine guides for children with ADHD/ASD
📏 Slant Boards	Helps with posture & writing focus

🔘 **Perfect For:** Children with *learning disabilities, visual impairment, ASD, CP, or ADHD*

⚡ 2. Mid-Tech Assistive Devices – *Smart Yet Simple* 💭 💡

These tools are **electronic but not too complex**. They offer interactive or audio-visual support and often improve **engagement, reading, or listening**.

📋 Key Features:

- Some power needed (battery or plug-in) 🔌

- Portable & classroom-friendly

- Requires **minimal training** to operate

✅ Popular Examples:

📌 Tool	💬 Use Case
🔊 Talking Calculators	Helps children with dyscalculia or vision problems
🎧 Audio Books	Support for dyslexia & reading challenges
📻 FM Systems	Amplifies teacher's voice for hearing-impaired students
🔍 Electronic Magnifiers	Enlarges printed material for low-vision learners

🕹️ Joysticks & Adaptive Mice   Improves computer access for children with motor issues

🎭 **Perfect For:** Students with *hearing loss, low vision, physical disabilities, or dyslexia*

🤖 3. High-Tech Assistive Devices – *Futuristic & Powerful!* 🚀 💻

These are **advanced, digital tools** that may use software, artificial intelligence, or specialized hardware. They significantly enhance **communication, writing, and access to digital content**.

🗂️ Key Features:

- High cost 💰

- Requires training & regular support

- Highly customizable for individual needs

- Best for **complex or multiple disabilities**

☑️ Popular Examples:

📌 Tool	💬 Use Case
🔘 AAC Devices (e.g., Proloquo2Go)	Non-verbal children communicate using pictures/speech
💻 Screen Readers (JAWS/NVDA)	Text-to-speech for blind/low-vision learners
🎙️ Speech-to-Text Software	Converts spoken words into text for students with writing disabilities
👁️ Eye-tracking Systems	Lets students control computers with eye movements
🧤 Smart Gloves / Haptic Devices	For students with mobility or sensory issues

🧤 **Perfect For:** Learners with *severe physical, communication, or visual impairments*

🎓 Real-Life Classroom Example:

Student	Disability	Device Used	Outcome
Riya (Class 2)	Cerebral Palsy	Speech-to-text software	Writes essays independently ✍️
Arjun (Class 4)	Hearing Impairment	FM System	Hears teacher clearly 👂
Priya (Class 3)	Autism	Picture Exchange Communication System	Expresses needs easily 🗣️
Aman (Class 5)	Blindness	Screen reader (JAWS)	Reads textbooks aloud 📖

❇️ Visual Flow Chart: Understanding the Levels

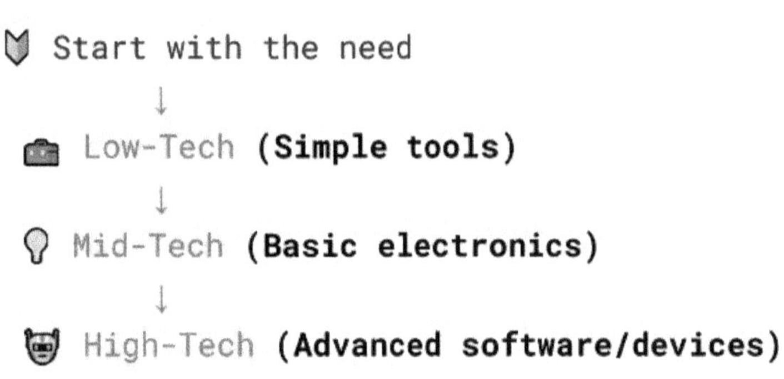

→ Choose the *least complex device* that solves the problem ☑️

📚 PYQ Corner

Q (DSSSB 2021):
Which of the following is a high-tech assistive device?
A. Braille Book
B. Talking Calculator
C. Eye-Tracking Device
D. Picture Cards
☑️ **Answer: C**

https://www.specialeducationnotes.in

❓ Practice MCQs

1. Which of the following is NOT a low-tech assistive device?
A. Pencil Grip
B. Braille Slate
C. FM System
D. Visual Schedule
☑ **Answer: C**

2. Audio books are categorized as:
A. Low-tech
B. High-tech
C. Mid-tech
D. No-tech
☑ **Answer: C**

3. Which student would most benefit from an AAC device?
A. A student who struggles with math
B. A student who is non-verbal
C. A student with hearing loss
D. A student with ADHD
☑ **Answer: B**

🗩 Quick Recap:

- **Low-Tech** = Simple, affordable (e.g., Braille, pencil grips)

- **Mid-Tech** = Basic electronic (e.g., audiobooks, FM systems)

- **High-Tech** = Advanced & digital (e.g., AAC, screen readers)

- Choose AT based on **student's needs, not the gadget's coolness!** 😄

🗩💬 *Augmentative & Alternative Communication (AAC) Devices*

For Children with Complex Communication Needs

✳ What is AAC?

AAC (Augmentative & Alternative Communication) refers to **all the ways** a person can
communicate without speaking.
It helps individuals who are **non-verbal**, have **limited speech**, or **unintelligible verbal output**.

◆ **Augmentative** = *Supports* existing speech
◆ **Alternative** = *Replaces* spoken communication

🎯 Who Needs AAC?

AAC is used by children with:

- **Autism Spectrum Disorder (ASD)** ✳

- **Cerebral Palsy (CP)** 🧍

- **Down Syndrome** ♡

- **Apraxia of Speech** 🖊

- **Traumatic Brain Injury (TBI)** ◐

- **Intellectual Disabilities** 🏛

💼 Types of AAC Systems

◆ Unaided AAC (No device needed)

Relies only on the user's body

👄 Method	📝 Description
🖐 Sign Language	Uses hands/fingers to express words
☺ Facial Expression	Smiles, frowns, and gestures to communicate feelings
👀 Eye Gaze	Eye movement to indicate choices

◈ Aided AAC (External tools/devices used)

⚙ Type	🖼 Examples
💼 **Low-Tech**	Picture cards, communication boards, alphabet boards
💡 **Mid-Tech**	Talking buttons, single-message voice devices
📟 **High-Tech**	Speech-generating devices (SGDs), AAC apps, tablets

📱 Popular High-Tech AAC Devices & Apps

💻 Tool/App	⚛ Features
👤 **Proloquo2Go**	Symbol-based speech output on iPad/tablets
☁ **Tobii Dynavox**	Eye-tracking AAC device for non-verbal users
🖥 **Avaz**	Widely used in India; supports multiple Indian languages 🔘
🐷 **GoTalk Devices**	Simple button-based devices for beginners
💬 **Speech Assistant AAC**	Android app converting typed text to spoken words

🔄 How AAC Helps in the Classroom

💡 Area	☑ Impact
👤 Communication	Children can express needs, wants & thoughts
☁ Learning Access	Supports participation in discussions & tasks
👥 Social Interaction	Builds friendships and reduces isolation
👤 Behavior	Reduces frustration & behavior issues due to communication barriers

🧩 Visual: AAC System Classification Chart

```
                  🧠 AAC SYSTEMS
                    /           \
           UNAIDED              AIDED
       (Signs, Gestures)       /   |   \
                             Low  Mid  High
                         (PECS) (Talking Button) (iPad Apps, SGDs)
```

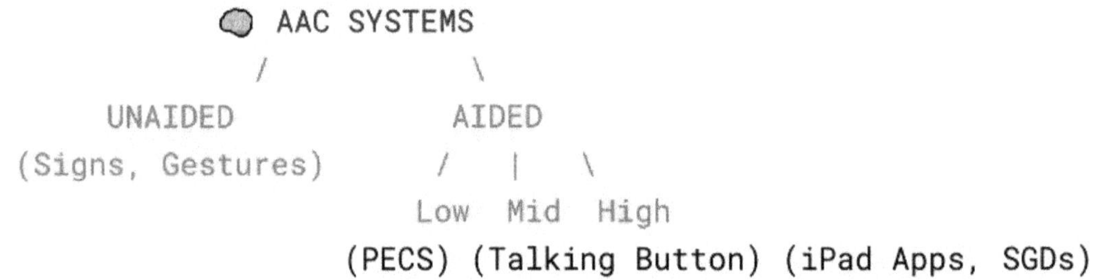

🎓 Real-Life Use Case

🧒 **Name:** Aarav (7 years old)
🧑 **Diagnosis:** Autism Spectrum Disorder
💬 **Challenge:** Non-verbal, unable to express needs
🛠️ **AAC Used:** Picture Exchange Communication System (PECS) → later upgraded to Proloquo2Go
🎉 **Result:** Now independently requests food, answers questions, and interacts with peers

---

📚 PYQ Corner

KVS 2020
Q: Which of the following is a high-tech AAC tool?
A. Braille Slate
B. Proloquo2Go
C. Sign Language
D. Visual Schedule
✅ **Correct Answer: B**

❓ Practice MCQs

1. AAC stands for:
A. Assisted and Augmented Communication
B. Augmentative and Alternative Communication
C. Adaptive and Assistive Communication
D. Alternative and Audio Communication
✅ **Correct Answer: B**

2. Which is an example of unaided AAC?
A. Communication App
B. Eye-tracking device
C. Sign Language
D. Talking Calculator
✅ **Correct Answer: C**

3. What is a key benefit of AAC in the classroom?
A. Makes students rely on others
B. Encourages silence
C. Improves communication and learning
D. Restricts interaction
✅ **Correct Answer: C**

📌 Quick Recap Box

📚 Key Point	✅ Summary
AAC Meaning	Communication without natural speech
Two Types	Unaided (no tools), Aided (devices)
Device Levels	Low-tech to High-tech
Classroom Impact	Improves speech, behavior, learning
Examples	PECS, Proloquo2Go, Tobii Dynavox

🌐 🤸 *Use of ICT in Special Education*

"When Technology Meets Inclusion!"

What is ICT?

ICT = Information & Communication Technology
 It includes **computers, internet, software, apps, projectors, smartboards, and AI tools** that enhance teaching and learning.

But in **Special Education**, ICT isn't just tech—it's **empowerment, independence, and access to learning** for ALL learners

---

Why ICT is a Game-Changer for Children with Special Needs

Need	ICT Solution
Can't read standard text	Text-to-speech tools & audiobooks
Struggles with writing	Speech-to-text software & typing tools
Needs structure & routine	Visual timetables & scheduling apps
Limited verbal speech	AAC devices, voice-output apps
Poor fine motor skills	Touchscreen devices, adaptive keyboards
Attention difficulties	Interactive lessons, educational games

---

Innovative & Modern Ways ICT Supports Special Education

1 Smart Classrooms for Special Needs

- Interactive Whiteboards → Visual, kinesthetic learners benefit

- Smart Projectors → Big visuals for low-vision students

- Tablets → Touch-based learning for CP/ASD students

2 Personalized Learning Software

- AI-driven apps adapt content to student's pace

- Tools like **Khan Academy Kids**, **ABCmouse**, and **BYJU'S** have inclusive features

3 Gamified Learning

- Apps like **ClassDojo**, **Endless Alphabet**, and **Toca Boca** keep learners engaged

- Rewards & points motivate children with ADHD, LD, and autism

4 Augmented Reality (AR) & Virtual Reality (VR)

- Makes abstract concepts real—ideal for **autism, dyslexia, and slow learners**

- Tools like **Tilt Brush** or **Quiver AR** make learning immersive

---

Cool ICT Tools in Special Education

Tool Type	Examples	Supports
Presentation Tools	Smartboards, Digital Charts	All learners
Learning Software	GCompris, JAWS, Bookshare.org	Blind, LD
Communication Tools	AAC apps, Avaz, Tobii Dynavox	Non-verbal
Mobile Apps	Proloquo2Go, Seeing AI, Voice Dream	Multiple
Web Resources	NCERT e-content, Diksha App	All-inclusive

Real-Life Impact Examples

Teacher Asha uses a **digital timer app** for her ADHD students to manage tasks without meltdowns

Rahul, a visually impaired student, accesses science books through **DAISY Reader**

Sara, with ASD, builds social stories using **Pictello App** to navigate real-life situations

Before & After ICT

Before ICT

Boring, one-size-fits-all lessons

Dependence on textbooks only

Limited communication for some kids

Difficulties in note-taking

With ICT

Custom, fun & adaptive learning

Interactive multimedia resources

AAC apps & speech tools open new worlds

Audio recording, screen readers

Practice MCQs

1. Which of the following is an ICT-based communication tool?
A. Braille Book
B. Picture Cards
C. Proloquo2Go
D. Pencil Grips
Answer: C

2. Which ICT tool benefits visually impaired students the most?
A. Talking Calculator
B. Screen Reader
C. AAC Button
D. Tactile Boards
Answer: B

3. Gamification in special education helps in:
A. Creating frustration
B. Reducing interest
C. Enhancing motivation
D. Causing distraction
Answer: C

🏫 🎖 *Role of Resource Rooms & Special Schools in Special Education*

"Bridges to Better Learning!"

❇️ What are Resource Rooms & Special Schools?

🏷 Term	📖 Definition
💬 **Resource Room**	A **supportive space** in a regular school where children with special needs receive **individual or small-group instruction** for a few hours a week.
🏫 **Special School**	A **separate school** designed specifically for children with disabilities, with trained staff and specialized curriculum.

💬🔧 Role of Resource Rooms – *"Support Within Mainstream"*

🎯 **Purpose:** To help children with special needs cope better in regular classrooms while still receiving special help.

📌 Key Features:

- 👥 **One-on-one or small group instruction**

- 💬 Focus on **individualized education plans (IEPs)**

- 📘 Provides **remedial teaching** (for reading, writing, math, etc.)

- ❇️ Improves **social integration** with peers

- 👤 Builds **confidence** & academic independence

---

https://www.specialeducationnotes.in

✅ Benefits of Resource Rooms:

📍 Area	✳️ Support Provided
📚 Academics	Extra practice & simplified explanations
🗣️ Language Skills	Speech therapy, language games
👥 Social Skills	Group activities, emotional regulation games
🎯 Attention Issues	Individual focus for ADHD/LD students
💬 Mild Disabilities	Students stay in inclusive settings with added help

---

👩‍🏫 Real Classroom Example:

🧒 **Child:** Aarav (Class 4)
💬 **Disability:** Specific Learning Disability (Dyslexia)
🏫 **Resource Room Support:** Receives reading & phonics intervention 3 times a week
🎉 **Outcome:** Improved fluency & confidence in class reading 📖✅

🏫🧒🏫 Role of Special Schools – *"Tailored Learning for Unique Needs"*

🎯 **Purpose:** To cater to children whose needs are too complex for regular schools (even with support).

📌 Key Features:

- 🧒🏫 **Trained Special Educators** for specific disabilities

- 💼 **Therapies available** (Speech, Occupational, Behavioral)

- 💬 Specialized teaching methods (e.g., sign language, Braille)

- 🧒🔍 Vocational training for life skills

- 📱 Focus on **holistic development** (academic + emotional + social)

✅ Benefits of Special Schools:

📍 Area	💥 How They Help
🗨 Severe Disabilities	Cater to ASD, CP, intellectual disabilities
👤 Communication	Use of AAC, sign language, PECS
🎓 Curriculum	Modified syllabus, slower pace
👦🔍 Vocational Skills	Prepares for semi-independence/livelihood
🧖 Therapy	Integrated into daily schedule

🧒 Real-Life Example:

🧒 **Child:** Meena (Age 10)
🗨 **Condition:** Severe Autism
🏫 **Special School:** Receives behavior therapy, sensory play, and basic literacy
🎉 **Outcome:** Improved interaction, ability to follow routines, and reduced aggression

⚖️ Resource Room vs. Special School: Quick Comparison

🔍 Feature	🗨 Resource Room	🏫 Special School
📍 Location	Inside a regular school 🏫	Separate institution 🏢
👦🎓 Student Type	Mild/Moderate disabilities	Moderate/Severe/Multiple disabilities
👦🏫 Staff	Special educator (part-time)	Full team of trained professionals 👤👥
📘 Curriculum	Same as general class (with help)	Customized curriculum 📚

⧖ Duration   Few hours per week   Full-time schooling ⏱

◎ Aim   Inclusion support   Specialized education & training

📚 PYQ Practice Time!

Q (KVS 2021):
Which of the following is a feature of a resource room program?
A. Full-day separate schooling
B. Therapy only, no academics
C. Individualized instruction in small groups
D. Focus only on life skills
☑ **Answer: C**

❓ Practice MCQs

1. Special schools are most suitable for:
A. Children with mild learning difficulties
B. All children
C. Children with severe/multiple disabilities
D. Children who dislike regular school
☑ **Answer: C**

---

2. A resource room provides support for:
A. Playing only
B. Therapy only
C. Inclusive education with extra academic help
D. Vocational training
☑ **Answer: C**

---

3. What is a key difference between a special school and a resource room?
A. Special schools are inside regular schools
B. Resource rooms do not use technology
C. Special schools offer a full-day, separate setup
D. Resource rooms have no educators
☑ **Answer: C**

      https://www.specialeducationnotes.in

🪨 Quick Recap Flashcard

📌 Point	🌟 Takeaway
Resource Room	Extra help within mainstream school 🏫
Special School	Full-time education in a specialized setup 🗂️
Focus of Resource Room	Academic & social support for inclusion 👥
Focus of Special School	Customized learning + therapy 🗨️💬

🪨💬 *Counseling Services & Family Support*

"Healing hearts 💚, building hope 🏠"

💢 Why It Matters in Special Education

When a child has special needs, **supporting the family is just as important** as supporting the child.
 Counseling and family support provide the **emotional, psychological, and educational tools** needed to create a nurturing environment at home and school.

😊🈯💫 What Are Counseling Services?

Counseling services refer to professional **guidance and therapeutic support** provided to:

- 💬 Children with disabilities

- 👨‍👩‍👧 Parents & caregivers

- 🧑 Teachers and school staff

Goal: Help everyone involved **understand, adjust, and grow together** 💪🌱

 https://www.specialeducationnotes.in

🗨 Types of Counseling in Special Education

✳ Type of Counseling	💡 Focus Area
🧒 Individual Counseling	Child's emotions, behavior, confidence
👨‍👩 Family Counseling	Parenting skills, family stress, expectations
🧑🏫 Teacher/School Counseling	Classroom strategies, inclusive practices, burnout care
👫 Group Counseling	Peer bonding, social skills training
🧘 Behavioral Counseling	Managing disruptive behaviors, positive reinforcement
🗣 Speech-Language Counseling	Language therapy, alternative communication strategies

🏠 ♡ Family Support: Backbone of Special Education

Supporting families means **empowering parents/caregivers** with tools, training, and emotional strength.
When families are strong 👉 **children thrive!**

🛠 Key Components of Family Support:

- 📚 **Parent Training & Workshops**
  ➤ Teaches behavior management, communication, and therapy techniques

- 🗨 **Awareness & Advocacy Support**
  ➤ Educating parents on rights, laws (like RPwD Act), and services

- 💬 **Support Groups & Networks**
  ➤ Parents connect, share, and motivate each other

- 🤍 **Home-School Collaboration**
  ➤ Joint planning of IEP goals, routines, and feedback

- 🧘 **Mental Health Support for Parents**
  ➤ Stress counseling, mindfulness sessions, emotional healing

👨‍👩‍👧 Real-Life Example

🧒 **Rohit**, a child with ADHD
👪 His mother joined a **parent training program**
💭 Learned how to use positive reinforcement and visual schedules
☑️ Result: Reduced tantrums, improved focus, and better bonding at home 🫂

🎯 Impact of Counseling & Family Support

🌱 Area	💥 Positive Outcomes
💭 Child's Well-being	Better emotional control, behavior, learning 💡
👨‍👩‍👧 Parental Confidence	More patience, understanding, and skill 💪
🧑‍🏫 Classroom Environment	Collaboration improves child's participation 📖
👥 Social Relationships	Improved peer interaction and self-image 😊
📙 IEP Success	More realistic and effective goals 🎯

💻 Use of Technology in Counseling Support

- 📱 Video Counseling (Tele-counseling for remote families)

- 🧘 Mental Health Apps (like Wysa, InnerHour for stress)

- ✳️ Parent Web Portals (share progress, behavior reports)

- 🧒🏫 Virtual Support Groups on Zoom, WhatsApp, Facebook

📊 Quick Recap Table

☑️ Key Area	📌 Summary
🎯 Counseling Types	Individual, Family, Group, Behavioral, Speech

⌂ Family Support Tools	Training, Support groups, Mental health care
💬 Goals	Emotional balance, better home-school connection
⬤ Tech Use	Online sessions, apps, virtual workshops
☑ Impact	Happy families = happier, successful learners 😀

📚 PYQ Practice

Q (DSSSB 2021):
What is the primary goal of family counseling in special education?
A. Increase academic burden
B. Teach sign language only
C. Support emotional and behavioral understanding
D. Avoid parent-school contact
☑ **Correct Answer: C**

❓ Practice MCQs

1. Which of the following is NOT a type of counseling?
A. Family
B. Peer
C. Group
D. Historical
☑ **Answer: D**

2. Parent support groups help in:
A. Competing with other parents
B. Isolating the child
C. Sharing experiences and gaining strength
D. Increasing academic pressure
☑ **Answer: C**

3. Which of the following strengthens home-school connection?
A. Ignoring parent suggestions

B. Joint IEP meetings
C. Avoiding feedback
D. Only teacher involvement
☑ **Answer: B**

7 Therapy, Treatment & Special Interventions

Children with special needs often face unique challenges that go **beyond academic learning**. For them, development is not just about reading and writing — it's about learning how to **communicate, move confidently, manage behavior**, and **express emotions**. 💬🏃💜

That's where **Therapy, Treatment, and Special Interventions** come into play. These are **specialized, personalized services** designed to support a child's physical, mental, emotional, and social development. Whether it's helping a child learn to speak clearly, walk steadily, calm their anxiety, or hold a pencil — these interventions play a **lifesaving role**. 🌟

🔍 What You Will Learn:

- ☑ Different types of therapies (Speech, Occupational, Behavioral, etc.)

- ☑ When and why treatments like medication or play therapy are used

- ☑ How **multidisciplinary teams** work together for a child's progress

- ☑ Real-life examples, tables, diagrams, and visual summaries for easy understanding

🚩 Why It Matters

Without proper therapy and support, many children may feel **left behind, frustrated, or misunderstood**. With timely interventions:

- 🎯 Their potential is unlocked

- 👨‍👩‍👧 Families feel supported

- 🏫 Classrooms become more inclusive

- ● Society becomes more accepting

☁ One Powerful Thought:

"Every therapy is a bridge — between a child's struggle and their success."

All Types of Therapy & Treatment for Special Needs Children

"Har therapy ek nayi roshni hai — towards better learning & living."

✳ Overview

Children with special needs often require **more than just classroom learning**. They may need **special therapies and treatments** that address:

- Emotional well-being ●
- Physical development 🏃
- Communication skills 🗣
- Behavioral issues 😳
- Sensory challenges 👁 👀

These services help the child function better at home, school, and in society. 🏫 🏠 ●

✨ Major Types of Therapies at a Glance

🏷 Therapy Type	🎯 Purpose / Focus Area
● Cognitive Therapy	Improve thinking, problem-solving, and emotional control

   https://www.specialeducationnotes.in

🪷 Behavioral Therapy	Correct negative behaviors; promote positive actions
🗣️ Speech Therapy	Improve communication, language, and articulation
✋ Occupational Therapy	Daily life skills (e.g., eating, dressing, writing)
🏃 Physical Therapy	Gross motor skills, balance, posture, muscle strength
👁️ Sensory Integration	Balance reactions to sensory input (light, sound, touch)
🧸 Play Therapy	Healing through play (for trauma, anxiety, ASD)
🎨 Art/Music Therapy	Emotional expression & relaxation through creative arts
💊 Medical Treatment	Medications for ADHD, epilepsy, anxiety, etc.
👨‍👩‍👧 Family Therapy	Help the family understand, support, and adjust

---

🧠 1. Cognitive & Behavioral Therapy (CBT/ABA)

- 🧠 CBT helps kids manage negative thoughts (used for anxiety, depression, SLD)

- 🪷 ABA (Applied Behavior Analysis) used for children with Autism to improve communication & reduce self-harm

☑️ Example:
A child with ASD learns to use flashcards to request toys instead of throwing tantrums.

🗣️ 2. Speech & Language Therapy

- Improves **speech clarity, language development**, and **social communication**

- Uses **sign language, PECS**, or AAC for non-verbal children

☑️ Used in: ASD, hearing impairment, Down Syndrome

✋ 3. Occupational Therapy (OT)

- Focuses on **fine motor skills**, like:

    o Holding pencil ✏️

    o Buttoning shirt 👕

    o Using spoon 🥄

- Also improves **sensory regulation**

✅ Used for: CP, Autism, ADHD, Sensory Processing Disorder

🏃 4. Physical Therapy (PT)

- Improves:

    o Muscle strength 💪

    o Balance ⚖️

    o Coordination 🤸

✅ Helpful in: Cerebral Palsy, Muscular Dystrophy, Spina Bifida

---

👂 5. Sensory Integration Therapy

- For kids who are over/under sensitive to sound, light, touch, etc.

- Uses tools like:

    o Weighted blankets 🛏️

    o Texture boards 🖐️

    o Sensory swings 🎋

✅ Used in Autism, SPD (Sensory Processing Disorder)

6. Play Therapy

- Helps kids express **fear, anger, or trauma** through games, dolls, drawing

- Builds trust, imagination, and coping skills

Used in ADHD, PTSD, emotional/abuse cases

7. Art & Music Therapy

- **Non-verbal expression** of emotions

- Improves mood, reduces anxiety, encourages communication

- Great for shy, anxious, or non-verbal kids

8. Medical Treatment (As needed)

- Includes medications like:

    - Ritalin (for ADHD)

    - Anticonvulsants (for epilepsy)

    - SSRIs (for depression)

- Must be used with **therapy and doctor's monitoring**

9. Family & Parent Counseling

- Educates parents about disability

https://www.specialeducationnotes.in

- Teaches them how to:

    - Set boundaries ⬡

    - Manage behavior at home 🏠

    - Support therapy goals ◯

✅ Builds better home-school coordination

📊 Visual Summary

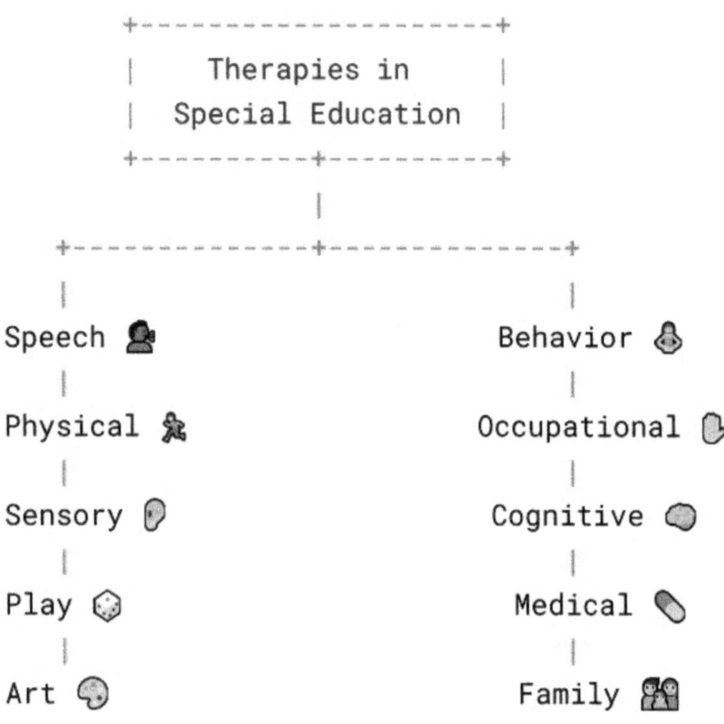

📚 PYQ / MCQs Corner 🎯

Q (KVS 2022):
Which therapy is most helpful for improving hand-eye coordination in a child with CP?
A. Speech Therapy
B. Occupational Therapy
C. Art Therapy

   https://www.specialeducationnotes.in

D. Play Therapy
☑ **Answer: B**

---

1. What does ABA therapy focus on?

A. Sensory play
B. Behavior change through reinforcement
C. Medication only
D. Musical skills
☑ **Answer: B**

---

2. Which therapy helps with sound sensitivity?

A. Art Therapy
B. Sensory Integration
C. CBT
D. Physical Therapy
☑ **Answer: B**

---

3. Speech therapy is mostly used for:

A. Walking balance
B. Muscle strength
C. Language and articulation
D. Vision correction
☑ **Answer: C**

🔍 Flash Recap

🔍 Need	☑ Therapy Name
👆 Fine Motor Skills	Occupational Therapy
👤 Communication	Speech Therapy
🧠 Behavior Control	Behavioral Therapy (ABA)
🏃 Gross Motor Strength	Physical Therapy

Sensory Processing   Sensory Integration

Emotional Expression   Art/Music Therapy

Seizures/ADHD   Medical Treatment

Family Understanding   Family Counseling

👶 *Individualized Behavior Plan (IBP) & Behavioral Interventions*

"Har baccha alag hota hai — uske behavior ka solution bhi alag hona chahiye." 🌱

📌 What is an Individualized Behavior Plan (IBP)?

An **Individualized Behavior Plan (IBP)** is a **custom strategy** designed to help children with special needs manage **challenging behaviors** in a structured, positive way.
It focuses on **what triggers the behavior, what the behavior looks like**, and **how to respond** in a way that helps the child learn better alternatives. 💬😊💭

🛠 **IBP is usually created when:**

- A child's behavior is **disrupting learning**

- There are frequent **tantrums, aggression, withdrawal**

- A child is not responding to general classroom rules

💭 Structure of an IBP

🔍 Component	📖 Description
🧩 Target Behavior	Specific behavior to reduce or improve (e.g., hitting, shouting)
📊 Baseline Data	How often behavior occurs before intervention
⚠️ Triggers/Antecedents	What happens *before* behavior (e.g., denied toy)

           https://www.specialeducationnotes.in

Replacement Behavior	What child will do *instead* (e.g., ask politely)
Reinforcement Plan	Rewards for good behavior (e.g., stickers, extra playtime)
Responsible Person	Teacher/parent who will monitor and guide
Review Date	When plan will be checked for progress

💡 Example of IBP

Target behavior: Throwing books when angry

Trigger: Gets difficult math questions

Replacement behavior: Ask teacher for help or take a break

Reinforcement: Gets star on behavior chart ✨

🔄 Behavioral Interventions – What Are They?

Behavioral interventions are **planned strategies** used to **change or guide behavior** in a positive way.
They are often based on **ABA (Applied Behavior Analysis)** and **positive reinforcement techniques**.

🎯 Types of Behavioral Interventions:

🖋 Technique	💡 Used For
✅ **Positive Reinforcement**	Giving rewards for good behavior (e.g., praise, tokens)
✖ **Response Cost**	Taking away privileges for negative behavior
🔄 **Token Economy**	Child earns tokens for good behavior, exchanges for rewards
🧍 **Self-monitoring**	Child tracks own behavior with checklists

| ⧗ Time-Out | Short break from activity after misbehavior |
| 👤 Social Stories & Modeling | Teaching behavior through stories or role-plays |

🏫 Where IBPs Are Used

- ◆ Inclusive Classrooms

- ◆ Special Schools

- ◆ Resource Rooms

- ◆ Therapy Centers

- ◆ Home Settings (with parent training)

🪨 Why IBPs & Behavioral Interventions Matter

- 🙂 Helps child regulate emotions and actions

- 🔔 Reduces classroom disruptions

- 👨‍🏫 Assists teachers with better classroom management

- 👥 Empowers parents to support from home

- 🎯 Improves academic and social outcomes

🎯 PYQs & MCQs Corner:

Q. IBP is mainly used to:
A. Teach language skills
B. Develop IEP goals
C. Manage challenging behaviors

D. Conduct IQ test

✅ **Answer: C**

Q. Which of the following is a part of an IBP?

A. School timetable
B. Baseline data of behavior
C. Eye test report
D. Daily homework log

✅ **Answer: B**

Q. What is the main goal of positive reinforcement?

A. To punish misbehavior
B. To increase desired behavior
C. To teach math
D. To test intelligence

✅ **Answer: B**

🔁 Quick Recap Table:

😕 Problem	🛠 IBP Solution
Hits when angry	Teach child to ask for help 🖐
Runs from classroom	Reward for staying in seat 🪑
Screams during task	Use calm-down corner 🧘
Refuses to do homework	Token system with small daily reward

🎇 One Powerful Thought:

"Behavior is a form of communication. IBPs help us understand the message behind the action." 💬

✳️ *Personalities in Special Education*

"Un logon ki kahani jo roshni ban gaye un bachon ke liye jinke liye duniya andhera thi." 💡

💭 Why Study These Personalities?

These educators, psychologists, and reformers played a **pivotal role in shaping** how children with disabilities are taught, supported, and understood. Their work:

- 🔍 Laid the foundation of **special education laws and practices**

- 🧩 Developed **learning theories and interventions**

- 🤍 Advocated for **inclusion and dignity of every child**

🧑 🏫 Key Contributors & Their Contributions

👤 Personality	🌐 Contribution to Special Education
Maria Montessori	Developed **Montessori Method**, focusing on **hands-on learning** and **individual pace**
Jean Marc Itard	Pioneer in special education; worked with the "Wild Boy of Aveyron" – used **behavioral methods**
Édouard Séguin	Introduced **physiological education** for children with intellectual disabilities
Anne Sullivan	Taught Helen Keller; known for **tactile teaching methods** for blind & deaf
Helen Keller	Advocate & inspiration; **overcame dual disabilities**; symbol of possibility 💪
B.F. Skinner	Introduced **Operant Conditioning** – basis for **ABA therapy** used in Autism
Lev Vygotsky	Theory of **ZPD (Zone of Proximal Development)** – foundation for **scaffolding** in special ed

Howard Gardner	Proposed **Multiple Intelligences Theory** – every child learns differently 🎨🎵📚
Dr. Vikram Patel (India)	Promotes **community mental health & inclusive education** globally
Anne Freud	Worked on **psychoanalysis of children**, child development

💡 Special Mention: Indian Contributors IN

👤 Name	✳️ Contribution
Dr. Mithu Alur	Founder of Spastics Society of India; worked on Cerebral Palsy awareness & inclusive schools
Dr. Sudha Kaul	Expert in **AAC devices** and special needs education policies
Dr. Asha Bhagat	Promoted vocational training for differently-abled youth
Javed Abidi	Disability rights activist – helped draft disability policies in India
Neelam Jadav	Pioneer in special education curriculum for Indian boards

📚 PYQs / MCQs Zone 🔥

Q. Who worked with the Wild Boy of Aveyron?
A. Maria Montessori
B. Jean Marc Gaspard Itard
C. Anne Sullivan
D. B.F. Skinner
☑️ **Answer: B**

Q. ABA therapy is based on the work of:
A. Piaget
B. Vygotsky
C. Skinner
D. Erikson
☑️ **Answer: C**

 https://www.specialeducationnotes.in

Q. Which Indian personality is associated with Spastics Society of India?
A. Dr. Asha Bhagat
B. Dr. Vikram Patel
C. Dr. Mithu Alur
D. Neelam Jadav
☑ **Answer: C**

🌐 Flash Recap Table

📖 Theory / Method	👤 Person
Montessori Method	Maria Montessori
ABA / Operant Conditioning	B.F. Skinner
Multiple Intelligences	Howard Gardner
ZPD / Scaffolding	Lev Vygotsky
Tactile Teaching	Anne Sullivan
Physiological Training	Édouard Séguin

✨ Inspirational Quote

"Alone we can do so little; together we can do so much."
— **Helen Keller** 🕊

8 Role of a Special Educator

"Na sirf shikshak, balki ek mentor, guide, therapist aur warrior!"

📖 Introduction

In the world of inclusive and special education, **Special Educators** are the real **changemakers**. They are **trained professionals** who understand the **unique learning styles, emotional needs, and developmental challenges** of children with disabilities.

Unlike regular teachers, special educators don't just teach subjects — they teach **life skills, emotional coping, communication,** and **confidence.**

They work as a **bridge between the child, the family, the school, and the larger society —** making sure that **no child is left behind.**

🎯 Why Are Special Educators Important?

- ✔ They make **inclusive education** successful
- ✔ Identify children's **strengths and needs**
- ✔ Create **Individualized Education Programs (IEPs)**
- ✔ Modify curriculum & environment to suit learners
- ✔ Work closely with **therapists, counselors, and parents**
- ✔ Provide **emotional and behavioral support**

🏫 Where Do They Work?

- 📍 Inclusive Classrooms
- 📍 Special Schools
- 📍 Resource Rooms
- 📍 Therapy Centers
- 📍 Home-based programs
- 📍 NGOs & Rehabilitation Centers

---

https://www.specialeducationnotes.in

🎗 Skills & Qualities of a Great Special Educator

💬 Quality	💬 Why It Matters
💗 Patience	Every child learns at their own pace
👁 Observation Skills	Helps identify needs early
💜 Empathy & Compassion	Builds trust with child and family
📚 Knowledge of Disabilities	For accurate planning and support
🔄 Flexibility	Adapts methods as per child's needs
👂 Listening & Communication	For collaboration with team & parents

---

🌟 One Thought to Begin the Chapter:

"A special educator doesn't just change lessons — they change lives." 🐞

🔍 *Identification & Early Intervention*

"Early help, better future!" 🌱⏳

📖 What is Identification?

Identification refers to the process of **recognizing signs of disabilities** or developmental delays in children at an early stage.
 Special educators observe **academic, behavioral, emotional, and physical patterns** to determine if a child may have special needs.

💬 Why Early Identification Matters?

- Helps in **timely support**

- Prevents future **academic and social gaps**

- Builds **child's confidence** from an early age

- Improves long-term **educational outcomes**

✏️ Tools Used for Identification

🧩 Tool / Method	📋 Purpose
✏️ Screening Checklists	Quick overview of developmental skills
🔘 Standardized Assessments	IQ, language, motor skills testing
👨‍🏫 Teacher Observations	Classroom behavior and learning patterns
🏠 Parental Interviews	Developmental history from home
👩‍⚕️ Medical Evaluations	Rule out physical/neurological issues

⚠️ *Note: Identification is not a diagnosis. It's the first step toward support.*

😊 What is Early Intervention?

Early Intervention refers to **targeted support and services** provided to children (typically 0–6 years old) **soon after identification**.
It includes therapy, counseling, educational plans, and family support to aid the child's development. 🔧

⚒ Key Components of Early Intervention

Area of Support	Example Services
Communication Skills	Speech Therapy
Motor Development	Occupational & Physiotherapy
Social-Emotional Skills	Play therapy, behavior modeling
Cognitive Development	Learning activities, special teaching
Family Involvement	Parental training, home strategies

🏫 Role of Special Educator in This Stage

☑ Observes child behavior in different settings
☑ Uses **screening tools & checklists**
☑ Collaborates with psychologists, doctors, and therapists
☑ Communicates findings to **parents sensitively**
☑ Designs **individualized early learning activities**
☑ Recommends **appropriate interventions & referrals**

💬 Real-Life Example:

A 3-year-old child shows delayed speech and avoids eye contact.
The special educator notices it during preschool activities and suggests an evaluation.
Early intervention through **speech therapy & social play groups** helps the child
develop better within 6 months. 💥

📚 PYQs / MCQs 🔥

Q. What is the ideal age group for early intervention programs?
A. 3-10 years
B. 0–6 years
C. 6–12 years
D. After diagnosis
☑ **Answer: B**

Q. Who plays the most important role in early identification of special needs?
A. School clerk
B. Subject teacher
C. Special educator
D. Principal
☑ **Answer: C**

Q. Which of the following is not a tool for early identification?
A. Screening checklist
B. Counseling session
C. IQ test
D. School uniform
☑ **Answer: D**

🌥 Quick Summary Chart:

🕘 Step	🔍 Action
🔍 **Identification**	Observe, record, and suspect a delay
👥 **Consultation**	Talk to parents, collect background
📄 **Assessment**	Use tools/checklists/tests
💼 **Intervention**	Start therapies & strategies early
🏠 **Family Support**	Train and involve parents

💭 *Collaborating with Parents, Teachers & Therapists*

*"A child with special needs needs a **team** — not just a teacher."* 🧩 👥

🗨 Why Collaboration is Essential?

Special education works best when **everyone involved with the child** is on the **same page** 📄✅
From home to classroom to therapy sessions — all need to share insights, strategies & progress to ensure a child's overall development 🧩

🧭 The Collaborative Triangle:

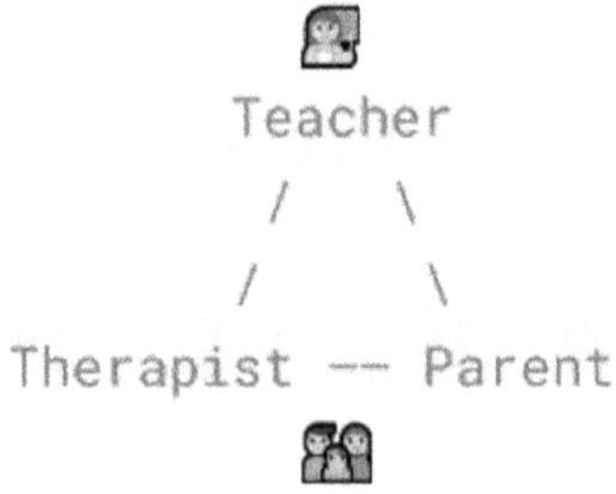

◯ **Special Educator is at the center**, connecting all sides to support the child.

🔍 Role of a Special Educator in Collaboration:

💼 Task	🎯 Purpose
👩 Parent Meetings	Share child's progress, listen to concerns
📐 IEP Coordination	Design personalized goals with team input
💗 Teacher Training & Guidance	Help general educators modify instruction
👤 Working with Therapists	Align classroom goals with therapy goals
🗂 Sharing Reports & Feedback	Track growth in all domains
🧍 Conflict Management & Support	Bridge communication gaps calmly

---

https://www.specialeducationnotes.in

👩‍👦 Working with Parents

- ☑ Involve them in **IEP meetings**
- ☑ Offer **home strategies** for behavior & learning
- ☑ Build **trust** through empathy and regular updates
- ☑ Respect their insights — they know the child best! 🤍

📋 *Example:*
A child is aggressive at school but calm at home. Parents reveal he calms down after a specific song.
→ Special educator uses **same strategy at school** 🎵👍

🧑‍🏫 Working with General & Subject Teachers

- ☑ Train them in **accommodations & modifications**
- ☑ Co-plan lessons with visual/auditory tools
- ☑ Explain child's needs in a **non-technical way**
- ☑ Promote a **positive & inclusive mindset** 💬📖

🎓 *Example:*
For a child with dyslexia, suggest the teacher use **audiobooks** and **oral tests** 🎧📋

🧑‍⚕️ Working with Therapists (SLP, OT, PT, Psychologist)

- ☑ Share classroom behavior to help therapy plans
- ☑ Implement therapy suggestions in daily routine
- ☑ Maintain a **progress notebook**
- ☑ Attend **case review meetings** 💭📊

⚕️ *Example:*
A speech therapist teaches signs to a child with autism. Special educator uses **same signs during story time** → Improve communication! 🧑‍🤝‍🧑💬

🔄 Communication Channels

📱 Tool / Method	📌 Purpose
Weekly Updates	Share child's goals & milestones
Emails / WhatsApp	Quick communication
Progress Reports	Academic + behavioral updates
Monthly Team Meetings	Align therapy + school plans
Sharing Photos/Videos	Show real progress moments

📚 MCQs / PYQs Section 🐣

Q. Who plays the central role in connecting parents, therapists, and teachers?
A. Principal
B. Counselor
C. Special Educator
D. Class Monitor
✅ **Answer: C**

Q. Collaboration ensures:
A. Faster curriculum completion
B. Exam preparation only
C. Holistic development of child
D. Use of standard textbooks
✅ **Answer: C**

Q. What is not a part of collaboration?
A. Feedback sharing
B. Conflict resolution
C. Isolation of team members
D. Co-planning of strategies
✅ **Answer: C**

https://www.specialeducationnotes.in

🫧 Summary Chart:

🫀 With Whom	🔲 Special Educator's Role
👨‍👧 Parents	Guide, counsel, train for home strategies
🧑 Teachers	Modify teaching, build inclusion
🧑 Therapists	Align therapy with classroom goals

📄 *Developing & Implementing Individualized Education Plans (IEPs)*

"One size doesn't fit all — that's why we have IEPs!" 🫧 ◎

🫧 What is an IEP?

An **Individualized Education Plan (IEP)** is a **customized learning plan** created for children with special needs.
It is designed **specifically to meet the unique educational, emotional, behavioral, and physical needs** of a child. 📚

IEPs are not just documents — they are **living blueprints** of a child's academic journey, revised and reviewed **regularly**.

◎ Goals of an IEP:

- 🔲 Support the child in achieving **realistic and meaningful goals**
- 🔲 Ensure **equal opportunity** for education
- 🔲 Provide a team-based, child-centric approach
- 🔲 Track **progress** and revise plans as needed

👤 Who Makes the IEP Team?

👥 Member	🧩 Role in IEP
👩‍🏫 Special Educator	Leads the plan creation & implementation
👪 Parents	Provide insights into child's strengths/needs
🧑‍🏫 Subject Teachers	Suggest accommodations in academics
👩‍⚕️ Therapists	Share therapy goals & strategies
🧠 Psychologist	Contribute assessment data
🏫 Principal/Admin	Approves resources & support

💬 *"It takes a team to build a dream!"*

📝 Key Sections in an IEP Document

📄 Section	🔍 What It Includes
📌 Present Level of Performance (PLOP)	Current skills & challenges
🎯 Annual Goals	Achievable goals within a year
💼 Special Services Required	Therapies, assistive devices, resource room etc.
🔄 Accommodations/Modifications	Extra time, oral tests, peer support
🗂 Review Plan	When and how progress will be tracked

🎓 Role of Special Educator in IEP Development

☑ Conduct detailed **observations and assessments**
☑ Lead the IEP meetings and **coordinate with team**

☑ Design **SMART goals** (Specific, Measurable, Achievable, Realistic, Time-bound)
☑ Train regular teachers to **implement accommodations**
☑ Record and review child's **progress regularly**

🛠 Examples of IEP Accommodations:

💭 Challenge	✅ IEP Strategy
Dyslexia	Audiobooks, oral instructions
ADHD	Short tasks, visual timetables
Autism	Visual schedules, sensory breaks
Hearing Impairment	Sign language, seating near teacher
Intellectual Disability	Simplified content, repetition

📚 PYQs / MCQs Section 🔥

Q. What is the main aim of an IEP?
A. To complete syllabus
B. To provide punishment
C. To meet child's unique needs
D. To compare children
☑ **Answer: C**

Q. Which of the following is a part of the IEP team?
A. Peon
B. Special Educator
C. Security Guard
D. Librarian
☑ **Answer: B**

Q. What is the ideal frequency for reviewing an IEP?
A. Once in 5 years

B. Weekly
C. Annually (or as needed)
D. Monthly only
☑ **Answer: C**

📊 IEP Quick Summary Table

🔍 Step	📕 Description
📌 Identification	Student referred due to difficulties
💭 Assessment	Formal/informal tools used
👥 Team Meeting	Goals, services, accommodations decided
📋 Documentation	IEP plan drafted and shared
🏫 Implementation	In-class support provided
🔄 Monitoring & Review	Progress tracked, plan adjusted

📚 *Providing Academic & Behavioral Support*

"Support isn't lowering the bar. It's giving the child a way to reach it."

🎓 1. What is Academic Support?

Academic support means **customizing teaching strategies and classroom materials** to help children with disabilities **learn better and stay engaged**.

☑ Key Academic Supports:

📌 Support Strategy	💡 Example
🗂 Simplified Content	Use easy language, break concepts into chunks

Multisensory Teaching   Use visuals, audio, hands-on materials

Time Accommodations   Extra time for tests & assignments

Modified Assessments   Oral exams, MCQs instead of long answers

Peer Tutoring   Pairing with supportive classmates

Goal: Make the child feel successful and included in learning.

🔍 2. What is Behavioral Support?

Behavioral support means helping children develop **positive behaviors** and reduce **problematic ones** through planned strategies.

💬 Why is it Needed?

- Improves classroom discipline

- Enhances peer relationships

- Boosts **self-esteem and emotional regulation**

⚙️ Types of Behavioral Supports:

🎯 Support Type	🧩 Strategy Used
☑️ **Positive Reinforcement**	Rewarding good behavior (stickers, praise)
Behavior Schedules	Structured routine to reduce anxiety
Redirection	Calmly shifting attention from disruptive acts
Social Stories	Short stories teaching expected behaviors
Behavior Chart	Visual tracking of daily/weekly behavior

👤🏫 Role of Special Educator:

🖼 Academic Role

🗨 Behavioral Role

Academic Role	Behavioral Role
Modify lesson plans	Create Individual Behavior Plans (IBPs)
Use assistive technology/tools	Model appropriate behavior
Give extra practice materials	Teach self-regulation techniques
Collaborate with subject teachers	Train staff for handling behaviors calmly
Monitor academic progress	Track behavior & give feedback

👁 Visual Infographic Idea

A 2-column layout showing:

🗨 Left: Academic Tools
🔖 Right: Behavioral Tools

Use icons like ✏ 📚 💿 for academics and 😊 😠 👟 for behavior

💬 Real-Life Example:

A child with ADHD finds it hard to sit still during a 40-minute lesson.
🔄 **Academic support**: Use short 10-minute learning activities + visuals
🗨 **Behavioral support**: Use a "focus timer" + reward for 10 minutes of staying seated
→ Results: Better focus + reduced disruptive behavior! 

📚 MCQs / PYQs Section 🔥

Q. What is an example of behavioral support?
A. Providing homework
B. Praising for calm behavior
C. Giving punishments

https://www.specialeducationnotes.in

D. Ignoring child's actions
☑ **Answer: B**

Q. What is peer tutoring?
A. Teaching other students
B. Student helping a classmate
C. Using computers
D. Calling parents
☑ **Answer: B**

Q. Which of these is not academic support?
A. Extra time
B. Social story
C. Simplified textbook
D. Visual aids
☑ **Answer: B** (Social story = Behavioral support)

📊 Summary Table

📖 Support Type	📌 Examples
Academic	Modified content, assistive tools, repetition
Behavioral	Praise, reward systems, structure, IBPs

⚖️ *Advocating for Inclusive Policies & Rights of Children with Disabilities*

"Disability rights are human rights." 💪 🙂

📌 What is Advocacy?

Advocacy means:

- "Speaking up"
- "Protecting rights"
- "Ensuring access & equality"

Special educators, parents, NGOs, and policymakers **work together** to promote the inclusion of children with disabilities in **education, society, and law**.

Role of Special Educator as an Advocate:

Area	Role Played
Schools	Push for inclusive classrooms & accessibility
Policies	Help shape child-friendly education policies
Legal Rights	Inform parents about disability rights & laws
Community	Reduce stigma and promote awareness
Administration	Demand proper implementation of IEP, RTE, RPwD

IN Key Policies & Acts in India for Children with Disabilities

Act / Policy	Main Provisions
RTE Act (2009)	Free & compulsory education for all children (6–14 years), including CWSN
RPwD Act (2016)	21 types of disabilities recognized; mandates inclusive education
National Policy for Persons with Disabilities (2006)	Focus on education, employment, barrier-free access
UNCRPD *(India is a signatory)*	Promotes dignity, equal opportunities, non-discrimination
Sarva Shiksha Abhiyan (SSA)	Inclusive education under RMSA

⬣ Issues Still Faced by Children with Disabilities:

◆ Lack of trained teachers
◆ Physical inaccessibility
◆ Social stigma & bullying
◆ Exclusion from mainstream education
◆ Denial of participation in activities

📢 *Hence the need for strong advocacy!*

⚒ Ways to Advocate Effectively

💭 Method	📌 Example/Action
📢 Awareness Campaigns	Workshops, school events, posters
👤 Parent Empowerment	Informing about rights & legal help
👤🏫 Teacher Sensitization	Trainings on inclusion & empathy
📜 Policy Recommendations	Suggesting changes in curriculum
🏛 Legal Support	Filing complaints in cases of exclusion
📱 Social Media Advocacy	Sharing stories, celebrating diversity

💬 Real-life Example:

👉 *A child denied admission due to Down Syndrome.*
👤 Special Educator informs parents about RPwD Act → Files a complaint with education board
☑ Result: Child admitted + school guided to follow inclusive norms

🎯 **Impact: One child included, a system changed!**

Q. Which Act recognizes 21 types of disabilities?
A. RTE Act
B. RPwD Act
C. SSA
D. NEP
☑ **Answer: B**

Q. What is the main goal of advocacy?
A. Charity
B. Punishment
C. Protection of rights
D. Academic excellence only
☑ **Answer: C**

Q. Inclusive education promotes:
A. Separation
B. Competition
C. Equality & Dignity
D. Fast learning
☑ **Answer: C**

📊 Final Summary Table

🧩 Element	☑ Inclusion Through Advocacy
🎓 Education	Barrier-free learning, inclusive schools
⚖️ Legal	RPwD, RTE, UNCRPD implementation
💗 Society	Awareness, stigma reduction
☁ Policy	NEP, SSA, resource allocation
👨‍👩‍👧 Families	Empowered with knowledge of rights

✨ Motivational Closing:

"The most powerful tool in special education is your voice — use it to open doors."

📙 *Conclusion: A Journey of Understanding, Inclusion & Empowerment*

As we come to the final pages of this book, let's pause and reflect...
We didn't just study **syllabus topics** — we explored **real lives, real struggles**, and **real hope** 🌿

💬 What You've Learned:

☑ Nature & Needs of Children with Disabilities
☑ Role of Teachers, Therapists, & Families
☑ Tools like Assistive Tech, IEPs, AAC Devices
☑ Rights, Laws & Advocacy that empower children
☑ Therapy, Interventions, and Love that heal

💡 The Heart of Special Education is:

"Not fixing the child, but fixing the system to welcome every child."

📣 Final Message to Readers (DSSSB/KVS Aspirants especially):

- You're not just preparing for a **job**, you're preparing for a **mission**

- Every classroom you enter may have a child **waiting to be seen, heard, and supported**

- With knowledge comes power — but with empathy comes **transformation** 🌏

     https://www.specialeducationnotes.in

🫂 Bonus Motivation for Exams:

🎯 Focus Area	🌟 Quick Tip
📚 Theory Questions	Use definitions + examples
☑ MCQs & PYQs	Practice regularly with reasoning
💭 Conceptual Clarity	Understand, don't just memorize
📝 Writing Answers	Use headings, bullets, flowcharts
💜 Stay Inspired	Remember WHY you chose this path

https://www.specialeducationnotes.in

⏎ Thank You for join us! 🙏📖

"Every child is a different kind of flower, and all together, they make this world a beautiful garden." 🌼🌸🌷

Now go out there — and make your classroom a place of light, love, and learning. 🏫💗
– With all heart, your study buddy (Preetam Dhayal) 🐶😄

https://www.specialeducationnotes.in

https://www.specialeducationnotes.in